This book belongs to:

....

....

....

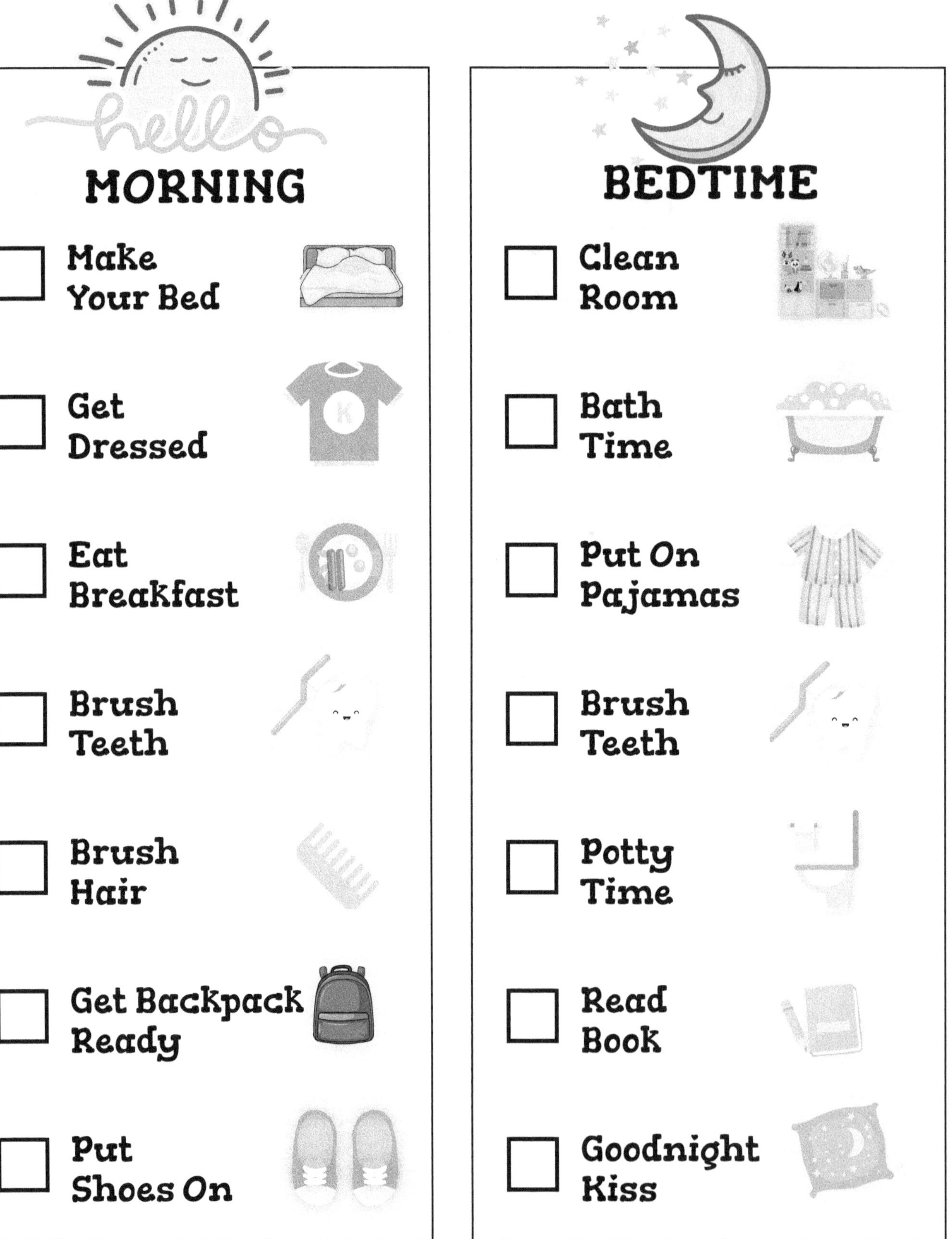

MORNING

- ☐ Make Your Bed
- ☐ Get Dressed
- ☐ Eat Breakfast
- ☐ Brush Teeth
- ☐ Brush Hair
- ☐ Get Backpack Ready
- ☐ Put Shoes On

BEDTIME

- ☐ Clean Room
- ☐ Bath Time
- ☐ Put On Pajamas
- ☐ Brush Teeth
- ☐ Potty Time
- ☐ Read Book
- ☐ Goodnight Kiss

Today Is:_______________

MORNING

- [ ] Make Your Bed
- [ ] Get Dressed
- [ ] Eat Breakfast
- [ ] Brush Teeth
- [ ] Brush Hair
- [ ] Get Backpack Ready
- [ ] Put Shoes On

BEDTIME

- [ ] Clean Room
- [ ] Bath Time
- [ ] Put On Pajamas
- [ ] Brush Teeth
- [ ] Potty Time
- [ ] Read Book
- [ ] Goodnight Kiss

MORNING

- ☐ Make Your Bed
- ☐ Get Dressed
- ☐ Eat Breakfast
- ☐ Brush Teeth
- ☐ Brush Hair
- ☐ Get Backpack Ready
- ☐ Put Shoes On

BEDTIME

- ☐ Clean Room
- ☐ Bath Time
- ☐ Put On Pajamas
- ☐ Brush Teeth
- ☐ Potty Time
- ☐ Read Book
- ☐ Goodnight Kiss

Today Is:_______________

MORNING

- ☐ Make Your Bed
- ☐ Get Dressed
- ☐ Eat Breakfast
- ☐ Brush Teeth
- ☐ Brush Hair
- ☐ Get Backpack Ready
- ☐ Put Shoes On

BEDTIME

- ☐ Clean Room
- ☐ Bath Time
- ☐ Put On Pajamas
- ☐ Brush Teeth
- ☐ Potty Time
- ☐ Read Book
- ☐ Goodnight Kiss

Today Is: ____________________

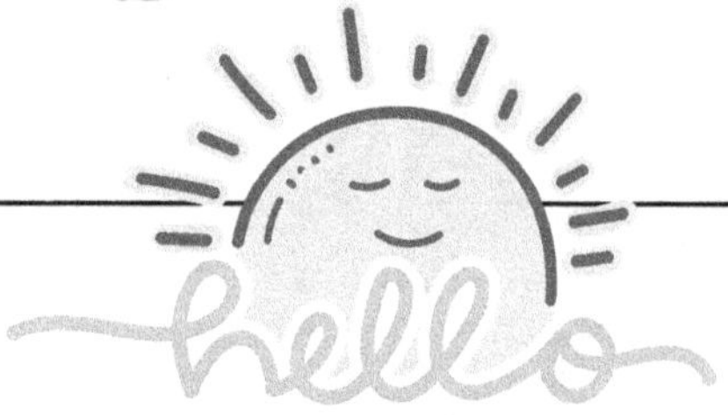

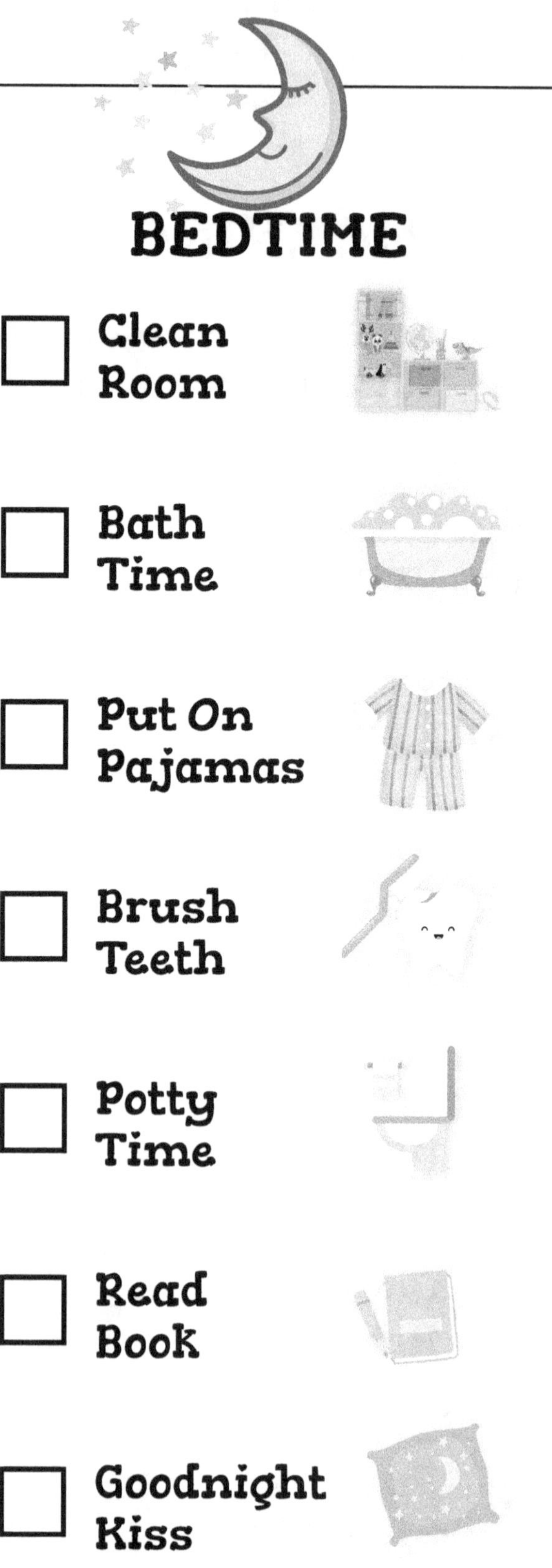

MORNING

- [ ] Make Your Bed
- [ ] Get Dressed
- [ ] Eat Breakfast
- [ ] Brush Teeth
- [ ] Brush Hair
- [ ] Get Backpack Ready
- [ ] Put Shoes On

BEDTIME

- [ ] Clean Room
- [ ] Bath Time
- [ ] Put On Pajamas
- [ ] Brush Teeth
- [ ] Potty Time
- [ ] Read Book
- [ ] Goodnight Kiss

Today Is:________________

MORNING

- [ ] Make Your Bed
- [ ] Get Dressed
- [ ] Eat Breakfast
- [ ] Brush Teeth
- [ ] Brush Hair
- [ ] Get Backpack Ready
- [ ] Put Shoes On

BEDTIME

- [ ] Clean Room
- [ ] Bath Time
- [ ] Put On Pajamas
- [ ] Brush Teeth
- [ ] Potty Time
- [ ] Read Book
- [ ] Goodnight Kiss

Today Is:_______________

MORNING

- ☐ Make Your Bed 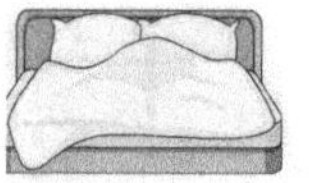
- ☐ Get Dressed 
- ☐ Eat Breakfast 
- ☐ Brush Teeth 
- ☐ Brush Hair
- ☐ Get Backpack Ready 
- ☐ Put Shoes On

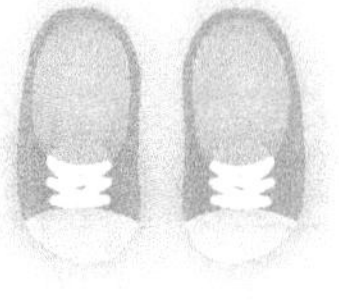

BEDTIME

- ☐ Clean Room 
- ☐ Bath Time 
- ☐ Put On Pajamas 
- ☐ Brush Teeth 
- ☐ Potty Time 
- ☐ Read Book 
- ☐ Goodnight Kiss

Today Is:________________

MORNING

- ☐ Make Your Bed
- ☐ Get Dressed
- ☐ Eat Breakfast
- ☐ Brush Teeth
- ☐ Brush Hair
- ☐ Get Backpack Ready
- ☐ Put Shoes On

BEDTIME

- ☐ Clean Room
- ☐ Bath Time
- ☐ Put On Pajamas
- ☐ Brush Teeth
- ☐ Potty Time
- ☐ Read Book
- ☐ Goodnight Kiss

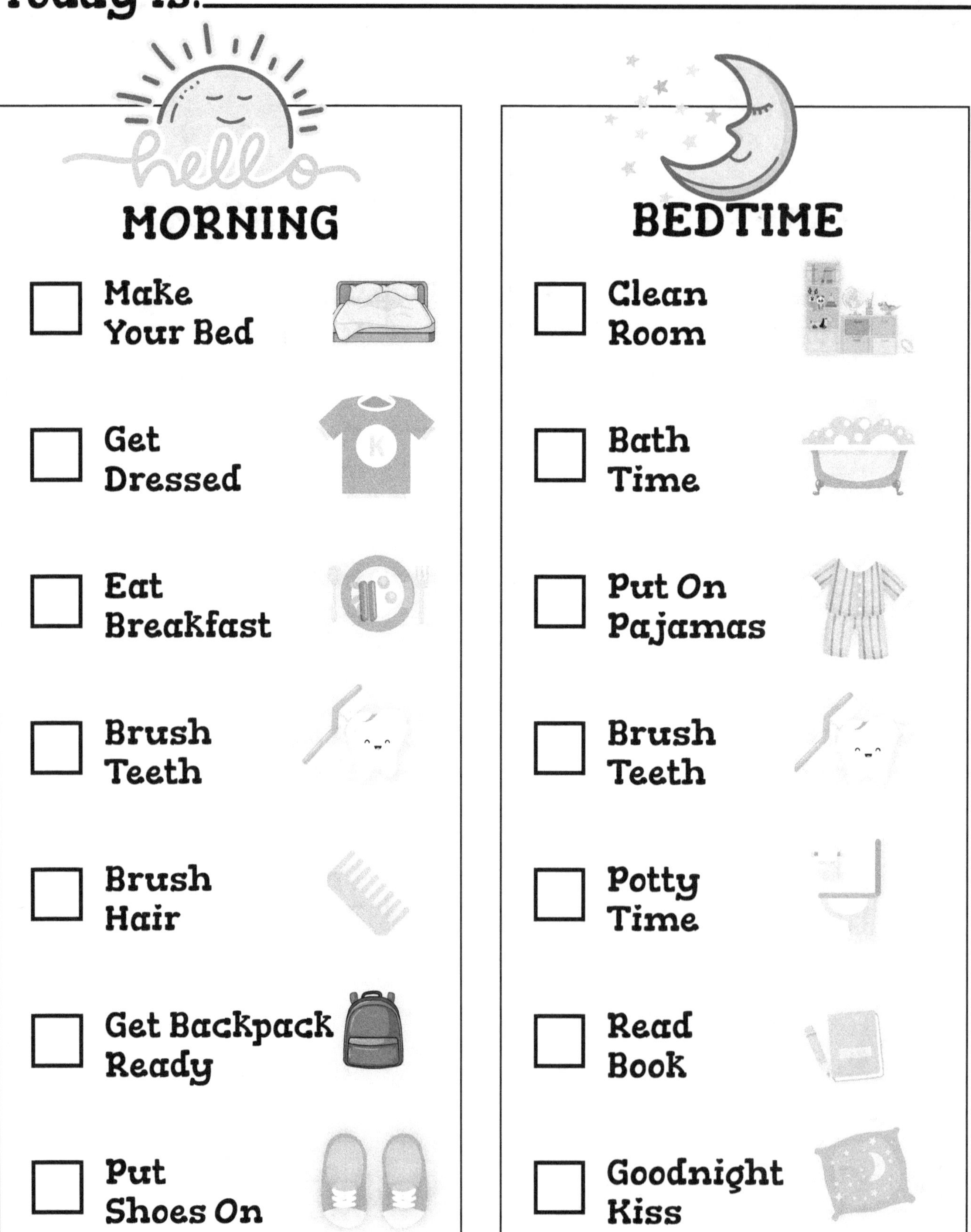

Today Is:_______________

MORNING
hello

Make Your Bed
Get Dressed
Eat Breakfast
Brush Teeth
Brush Hair
Get Backpack Ready
Put Shoes On

BEDTIME

Clean Room
Bath Time
Put On Pajamas
Brush Teeth
Potty Time
Read Book
Goodnight Kiss

Today Is:___________

MORNING

☐ Make Your Bed

☐ Get Dressed

☐ Eat Breakfast

☐ Brush Teeth

☐ Brush Hair

☐ Get Backpack Ready

☐ Put Shoes On

BEDTIME

☐ Clean Room

☐ Bath Time

☐ Put On Pajamas

☐ Brush Teeth

☐ Potty Time

☐ Read Book

☐ Goodnight Kiss

Today Is:_______________

MORNING

- ☐ **Make Your Bed** 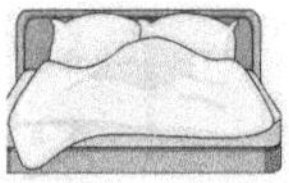
- ☐ **Get Dressed** 
- ☐ **Eat Breakfast** 
- ☐ **Brush Teeth** 
- ☐ **Brush Hair**
- ☐ **Get Backpack Ready** 
- ☐ **Put Shoes On**

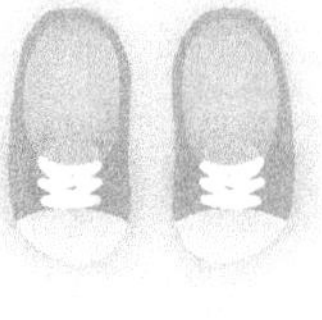

BEDTIME

- ☐ **Clean Room**
- ☐ **Bath Time**
- ☐ **Put On Pajamas**
- ☐ **Brush Teeth**
- ☐ **Potty Time**
- ☐ **Read Book**
- ☐ **Goodnight Kiss**

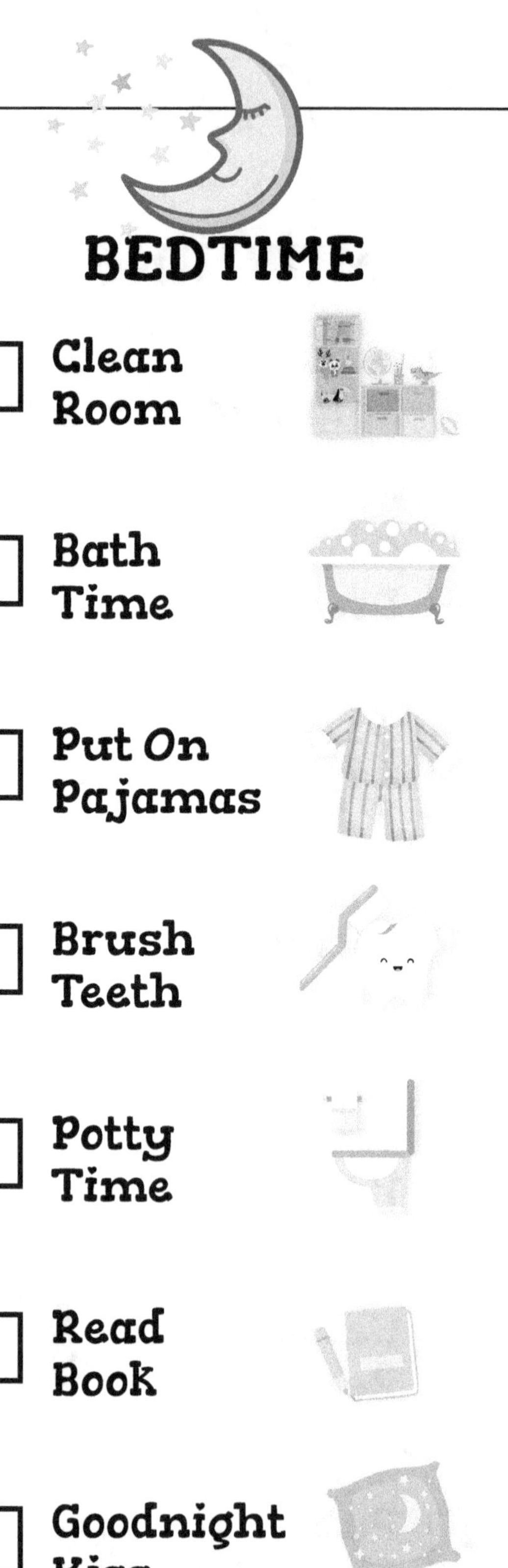

Today Is:________________________

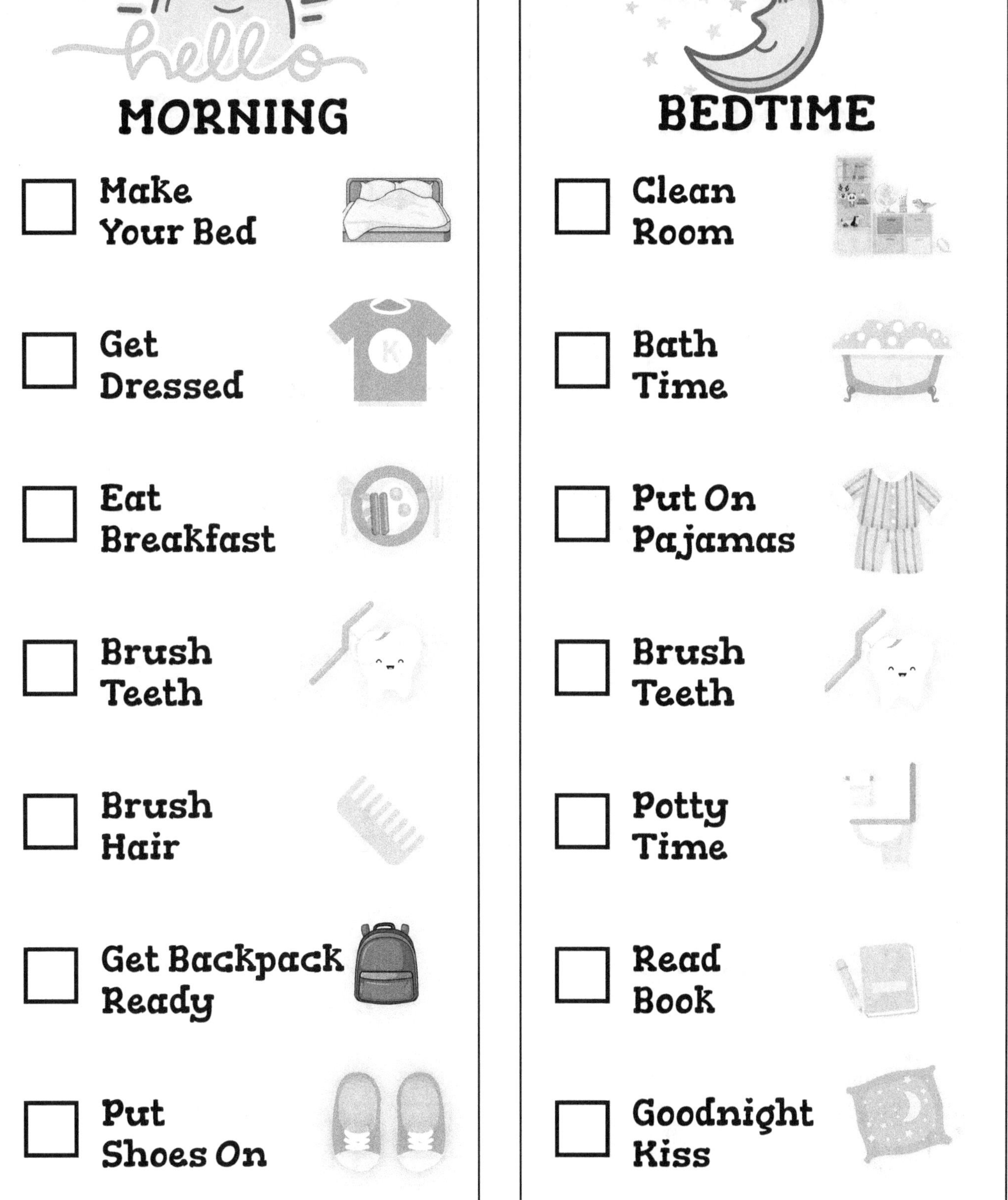

MORNING

- ☐ Make Your Bed
- ☐ Get Dressed
- ☐ Eat Breakfast
- ☐ Brush Teeth
- ☐ Brush Hair
- ☐ Get Backpack Ready
- ☐ Put Shoes On

BEDTIME

- ☐ Clean Room
- ☐ Bath Time
- ☐ Put On Pajamas
- ☐ Brush Teeth
- ☐ Potty Time
- ☐ Read Book
- ☐ Goodnight Kiss

Today Is: ____________________

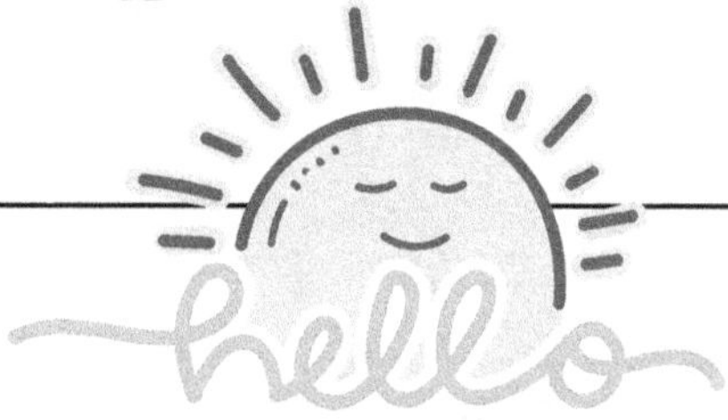

MORNING

- [ ] Make Your Bed 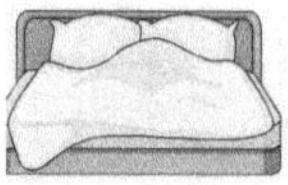
- [ ] Get Dressed 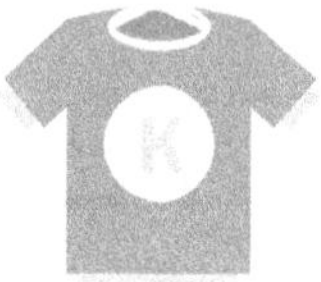
- [ ] Eat Breakfast 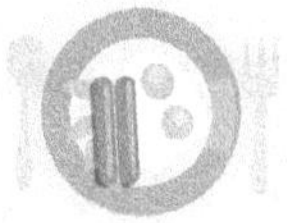
- [ ] Brush Teeth 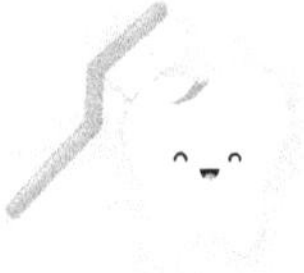
- [ ] Brush Hair
- [ ] Get Backpack Ready 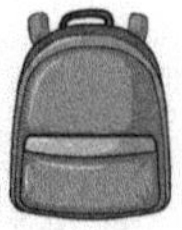
- [ ] Put Shoes On 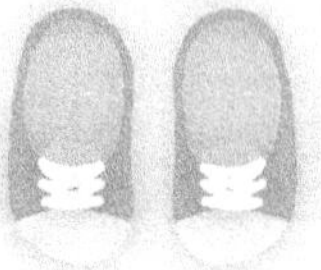

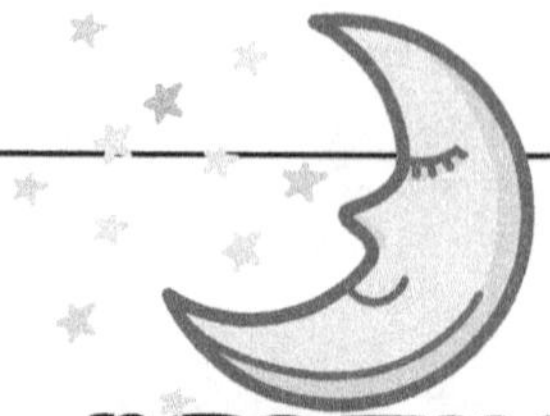

BEDTIME

- [ ] Clean Room 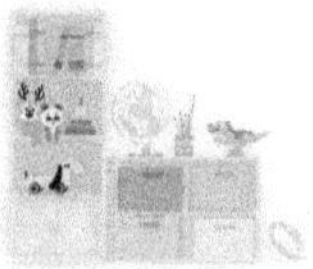
- [ ] Bath Time 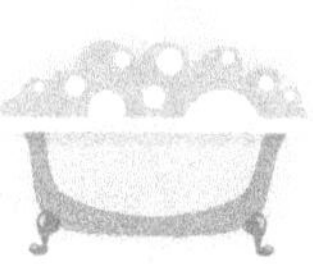
- [ ] Put On Pajamas 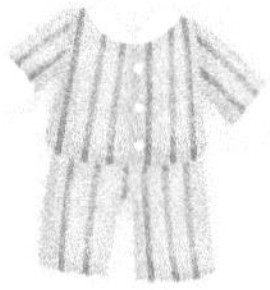
- [ ] Brush Teeth 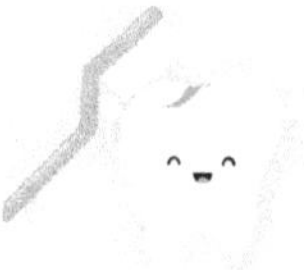
- [ ] Potty Time
- [ ] Read Book
- [ ] Goodnight Kiss 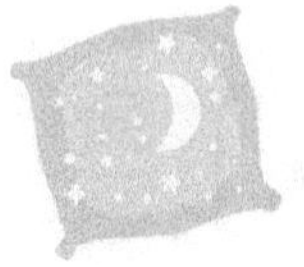

MORNING

- ☐ Make Your Bed
- ☐ Get Dressed
- ☐ Eat Breakfast
- ☐ Brush Teeth
- ☐ Brush Hair
- ☐ Get Backpack Ready
- ☐ Put Shoes On

BEDTIME

- ☐ Clean Room
- ☐ Bath Time
- ☐ Put On Pajamas
- ☐ Brush Teeth
- ☐ Potty Time
- ☐ Read Book
- ☐ Goodnight Kiss

MORNING

- ☐ Make Your Bed 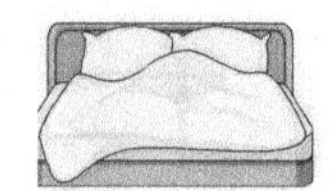
- ☐ Get Dressed 
- ☐ Eat Breakfast 
- ☐ Brush Teeth 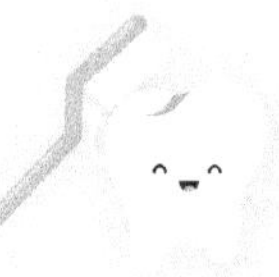
- ☐ Brush Hair 
- ☐ Get Backpack Ready 
- ☐ Put Shoes On 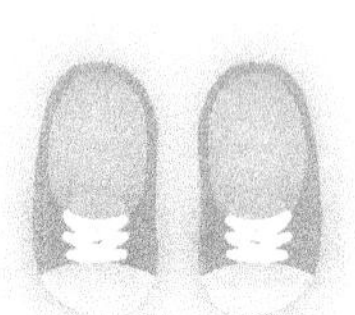

BEDTIME

- ☐ Clean Room 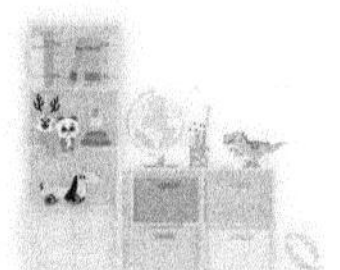
- ☐ Bath Time 
- ☐ Put On Pajamas 
- ☐ Brush Teeth 
- ☐ Potty Time 
- ☐ Read Book 
- ☐ Goodnight Kiss 

Today Is:_______________

MORNING

- ☐ Make Your Bed
- ☐ Get Dressed
- ☐ Eat Breakfast
- ☐ Brush Teeth
- ☐ Brush Hair
- ☐ Get Backpack Ready
- ☐ Put Shoes On

BEDTIME

- ☐ Clean Room
- ☐ Bath Time
- ☐ Put On Pajamas
- ☐ Brush Teeth
- ☐ Potty Time
- ☐ Read Book
- ☐ Goodnight Kiss

MORNING

- ☐ Make Your Bed
- ☐ Get Dressed
- ☐ Eat Breakfast
- ☐ Brush Teeth
- ☐ Brush Hair
- ☐ Get Backpack Ready
- ☐ Put Shoes On

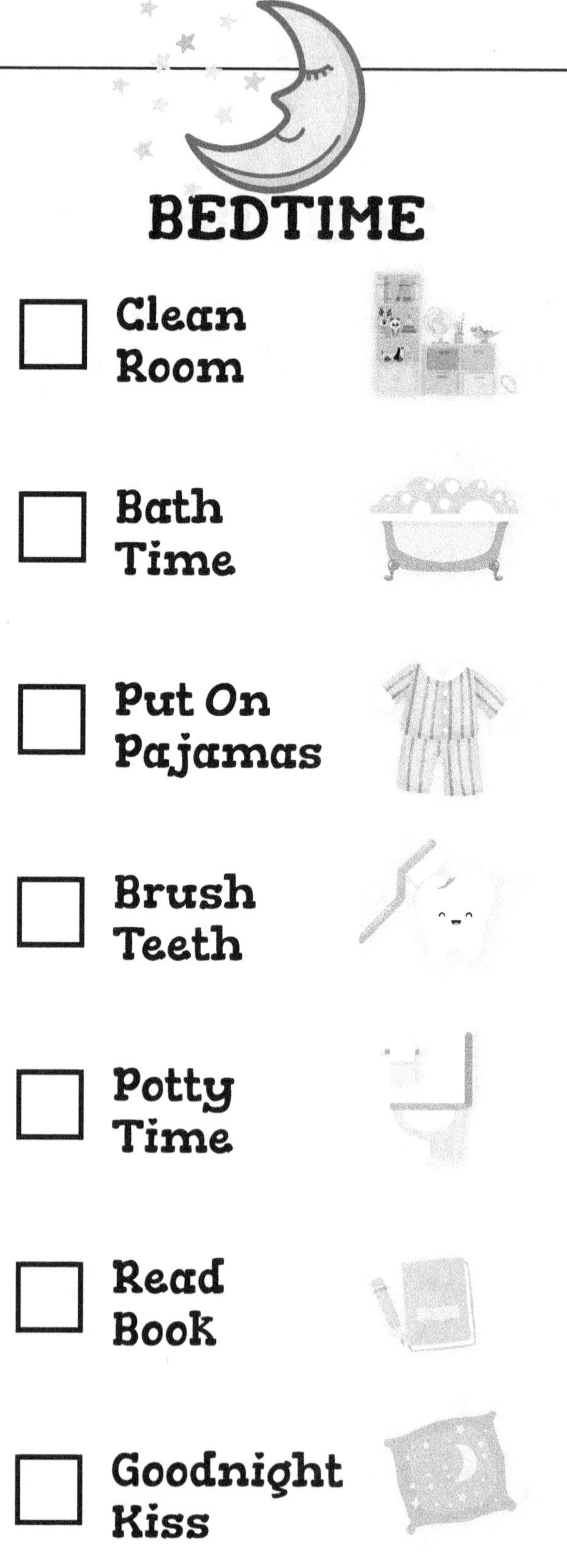

BEDTIME

- ☐ Clean Room
- ☐ Bath Time
- ☐ Put On Pajamas
- ☐ Brush Teeth
- ☐ Potty Time
- ☐ Read Book
- ☐ Goodnight Kiss

Today Is:_______________

MORNING

- ☐ Make Your Bed
- ☐ Get Dressed
- ☐ Eat Breakfast
- ☐ Brush Teeth
- ☐ Brush Hair
- ☐ Get Backpack Ready
- ☐ Put Shoes On

BEDTIME

- ☐ Clean Room
- ☐ Bath Time
- ☐ Put On Pajamas
- ☐ Brush Teeth
- ☐ Potty Time
- ☐ Read Book
- ☐ Goodnight Kiss

Today Is:____________________

MORNING

- ☐ Make Your Bed 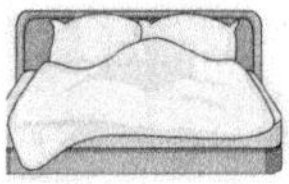
- ☐ Get Dressed 
- ☐ Eat Breakfast 
- ☐ Brush Teeth 
- ☐ Brush Hair
- ☐ Get Backpack Ready 
- ☐ Put Shoes On

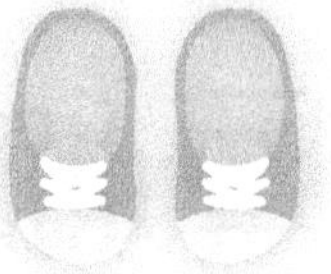

BEDTIME

- ☐ Clean Room
- ☐ Bath Time
- ☐ Put On Pajamas
- ☐ Brush Teeth
- ☐ Potty Time
- ☐ Read Book
- ☐ Goodnight Kiss

MORNING

- [ ] Make Your Bed
- [ ] Get Dressed
- [ ] Eat Breakfast
- [ ] Brush Teeth
- [ ] Brush Hair
- [ ] Get Backpack Ready
- [ ] Put Shoes On

BEDTIME

- [ ] Clean Room
- [ ] Bath Time
- [ ] Put On Pajamas
- [ ] Brush Teeth
- [ ] Potty Time
- [ ] Read Book
- [ ] Goodnight Kiss

Today Is:____________

MORNING

- ☐ Make Your Bed
- ☐ Get Dressed
- ☐ Eat Breakfast
- ☐ Brush Teeth
- ☐ Brush Hair
- ☐ Get Backpack Ready
- ☐ Put Shoes On

BEDTIME

- ☐ Clean Room
- ☐ Bath Time
- ☐ Put On Pajamas
- ☐ Brush Teeth
- ☐ Potty Time
- ☐ Read Book
- ☐ Goodnight Kiss

Today Is:_______________

MORNING	BEDTIME

MORNING

- ☐ Make Your Bed
- ☐ Get Dressed
- ☐ Eat Breakfast
- ☐ Brush Teeth
- ☐ Brush Hair
- ☐ Get Backpack Ready
- ☐ Put Shoes On

BEDTIME

- ☐ Clean Room
- ☐ Bath Time
- ☐ Put On Pajamas
- ☐ Brush Teeth
- ☐ Potty Time
- ☐ Read Book
- ☐ Goodnight Kiss

MORNING

- ☐ Make Your Bed 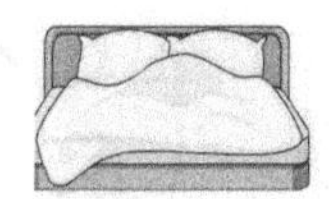
- ☐ Get Dressed 
- ☐ Eat Breakfast 
- ☐ Brush Teeth 
- ☐ Brush Hair 
- ☐ Get Backpack Ready 
- ☐ Put Shoes On 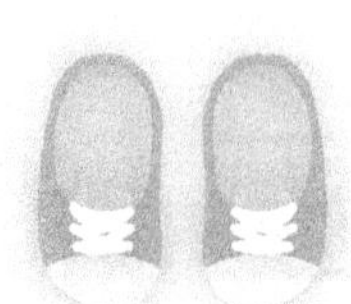

BEDTIME

- ☐ Clean Room 
- ☐ Bath Time 
- ☐ Put On Pajamas 
- ☐ Brush Teeth 
- ☐ Potty Time 
- ☐ Read Book 
- ☐ Goodnight Kiss 

Today Is:________________

MORNING

- ☐ Make Your Bed
- ☐ Get Dressed
- ☐ Eat Breakfast
- ☐ Brush Teeth
- ☐ Brush Hair
- ☐ Get Backpack Ready
- ☐ Put Shoes On

BEDTIME

- ☐ Clean Room
- ☐ Bath Time
- ☐ Put On Pajamas
- ☐ Brush Teeth
- ☐ Potty Time
- ☐ Read Book
- ☐ Goodnight Kiss

Today Is:________________

MORNING

- ☐ Make Your Bed 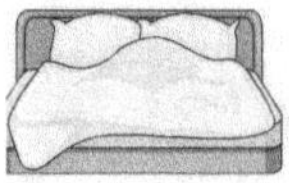
- ☐ Get Dressed 
- ☐ Eat Breakfast 
- ☐ Brush Teeth 
- ☐ Brush Hair
- ☐ Get Backpack Ready 
- ☐ Put Shoes On

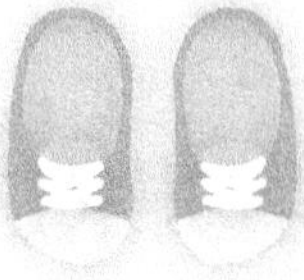

BEDTIME

- ☐ Clean Room 
- ☐ Bath Time 
- ☐ Put On Pajamas 
- ☐ Brush Teeth 
- ☐ Potty Time
- ☐ Read Book 
- ☐ Goodnight Kiss

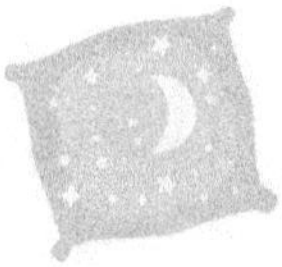

Today Is:__________________

MORNING

- ☐ Make Your Bed 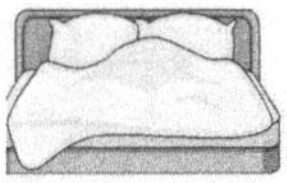
- ☐ Get Dressed 
- ☐ Eat Breakfast 
- ☐ Brush Teeth 
- ☐ Brush Hair
- ☐ Get Backpack Ready 
- ☐ Put Shoes On

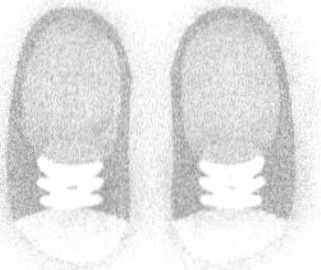

BEDTIME

- ☐ Clean Room 
- ☐ Bath Time 
- ☐ Put On Pajamas 
- ☐ Brush Teeth 
- ☐ Potty Time
- ☐ Read Book
- ☐ Goodnight Kiss

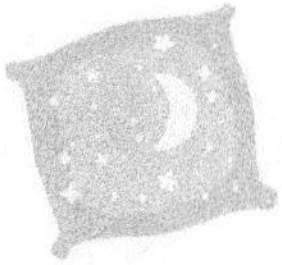

Today Is:____________________

MORNING

- [ ] Make Your Bed 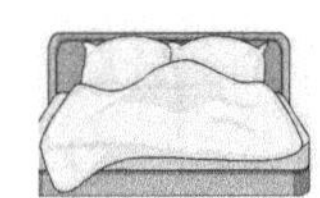
- [ ] Get Dressed 
- [ ] Eat Breakfast 
- [ ] Brush Teeth 
- [ ] Brush Hair 
- [ ] Get Backpack Ready 
- [ ] Put Shoes On 

BEDTIME

- [ ] Clean Room 
- [ ] Bath Time 
- [ ] Put On Pajamas 
- [ ] Brush Teeth 
- [ ] Potty Time 
- [ ] Read Book 
- [ ] Goodnight Kiss 

Today Is:_______________

MORNING

- ☐ Make Your Bed
- ☐ Get Dressed
- ☐ Eat Breakfast
- ☐ Brush Teeth
- ☐ Brush Hair
- ☐ Get Backpack Ready
- ☐ Put Shoes On

BEDTIME

- ☐ Clean Room
- ☐ Bath Time
- ☐ Put On Pajamas
- ☐ Brush Teeth
- ☐ Potty Time
- ☐ Read Book
- ☐ Goodnight Kiss

Today Is:_______________

MORNING

- ☐ Make Your Bed 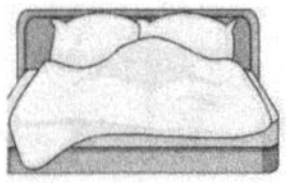
- ☐ Get Dressed 
- ☐ Eat Breakfast 
- ☐ Brush Teeth 
- ☐ Brush Hair
- ☐ Get Backpack Ready 
- ☐ Put Shoes On

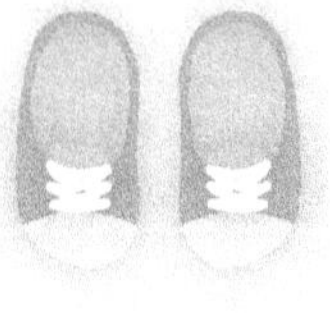

BEDTIME

- ☐ Clean Room
- ☐ Bath Time
- ☐ Put On Pajamas
- ☐ Brush Teeth
- ☐ Potty Time
- ☐ Read Book
- ☐ Goodnight Kiss

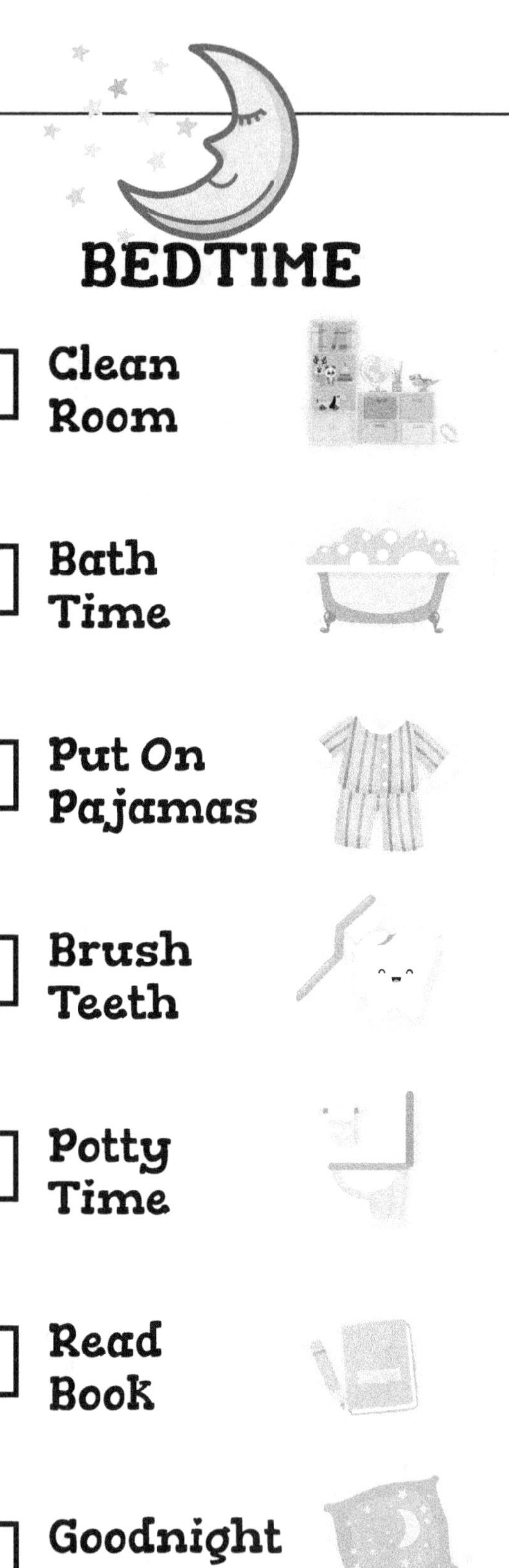

Today Is:_______________

MORNING

- ☐ Make Your Bed
- ☐ Get Dressed
- ☐ Eat Breakfast
- ☐ Brush Teeth
- ☐ Brush Hair
- ☐ Get Backpack Ready
- ☐ Put Shoes On

BEDTIME

- ☐ Clean Room
- ☐ Bath Time
- ☐ Put On Pajamas
- ☐ Brush Teeth
- ☐ Potty Time
- ☐ Read Book
- ☐ Goodnight Kiss

Today Is:_______________

MORNING

- ☐ Make Your Bed 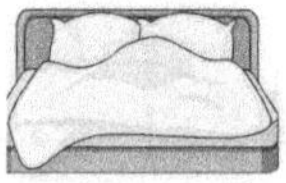
- ☐ Get Dressed 
- ☐ Eat Breakfast 
- ☐ Brush Teeth 
- ☐ Brush Hair
- ☐ Get Backpack Ready 
- ☐ Put Shoes On

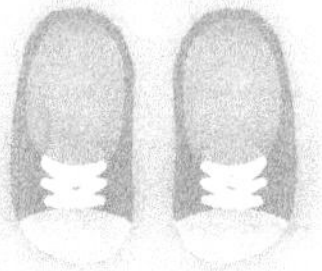

BEDTIME

- ☐ Clean Room 
- ☐ Bath Time 
- ☐ Put On Pajamas 
- ☐ Brush Teeth 
- ☐ Potty Time
- ☐ Read Book 
- ☐ Goodnight Kiss

MORNING

- [ ] Make Your Bed
- [ ] Get Dressed
- [ ] Eat Breakfast
- [ ] Brush Teeth
- [ ] Brush Hair
- [ ] Get Backpack Ready
- [ ] Put Shoes On

BEDTIME

- [ ] Clean Room
- [ ] Bath Time
- [ ] Put On Pajamas
- [ ] Brush Teeth
- [ ] Potty Time
- [ ] Read Book
- [ ] Goodnight Kiss

Today Is:＿＿＿＿＿＿＿＿＿＿＿

MORNING

- ☐ Make Your Bed
- ☐ Get Dressed
- ☐ Eat Breakfast
- ☐ Brush Teeth
- ☐ Brush Hair
- ☐ Get Backpack Ready
- ☐ Put Shoes On

BEDTIME

- ☐ Clean Room
- ☐ Bath Time
- ☐ Put On Pajamas
- ☐ Brush Teeth
- ☐ Potty Time
- ☐ Read Book
- ☐ Goodnight Kiss

Today Is:___________________

MORNING

- ☐ Make Your Bed 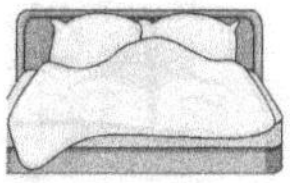
- ☐ Get Dressed 
- ☐ Eat Breakfast 
- ☐ Brush Teeth 
- ☐ Brush Hair
- ☐ Get Backpack Ready 
- ☐ Put Shoes On

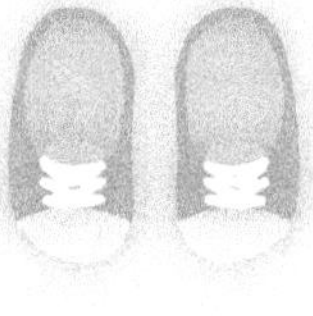

BEDTIME

- ☐ Clean Room 
- ☐ Bath Time 
- ☐ Put On Pajamas 
- ☐ Brush Teeth 
- ☐ Potty Time
- ☐ Read Book
- ☐ Goodnight Kiss

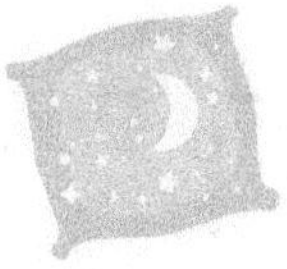

Today Is:_______________________

MORNING

- ☐ Make Your Bed 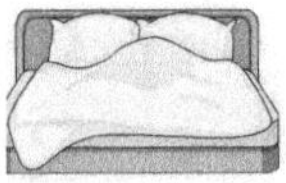
- ☐ Get Dressed 
- ☐ Eat Breakfast 
- ☐ Brush Teeth 
- ☐ Brush Hair
- ☐ Get Backpack Ready 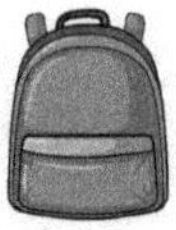
- ☐ Put Shoes On

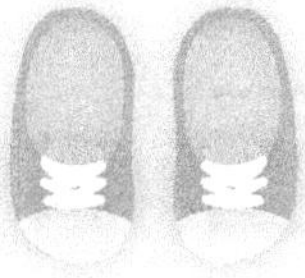

BEDTIME

- ☐ Clean Room 
- ☐ Bath Time 
- ☐ Put On Pajamas 
- ☐ Brush Teeth 
- ☐ Potty Time
- ☐ Read Book 
- ☐ Goodnight Kiss

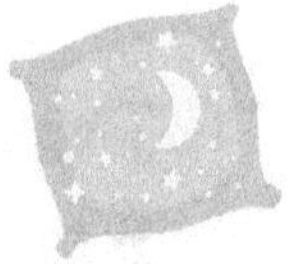

Today Is:_______________

MORNING

- ☐ Make Your Bed
- ☐ Get Dressed
- ☐ Eat Breakfast
- ☐ Brush Teeth
- ☐ Brush Hair
- ☐ Get Backpack Ready
- ☐ Put Shoes On

BEDTIME

- ☐ Clean Room
- ☐ Bath Time
- ☐ Put On Pajamas
- ☐ Brush Teeth
- ☐ Potty Time
- ☐ Read Book
- ☐ Goodnight Kiss

Today Is:________________

MORNING

- ☐ Make Your Bed
- ☐ Get Dressed
- ☐ Eat Breakfast
- ☐ Brush Teeth
- ☐ Brush Hair
- ☐ Get Backpack Ready 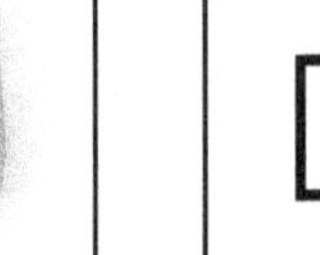
- ☐ Put Shoes On

BEDTIME

- ☐ Clean Room
- ☐ Bath Time
- ☐ Put On Pajamas
- ☐ Brush Teeth
- ☐ Potty Time
- ☐ Read Book
- ☐ Goodnight Kiss

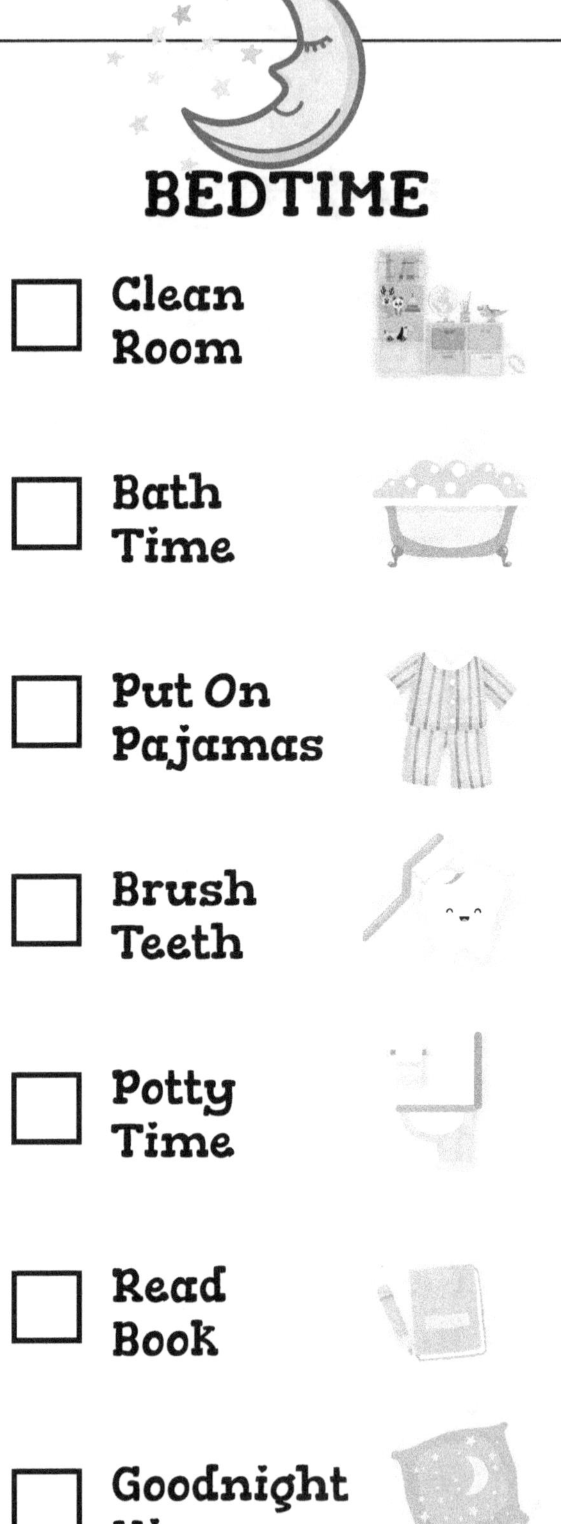

Today Is:_______________

MORNING

- ☐ Make Your Bed
- ☐ Get Dressed
- ☐ Eat Breakfast
- ☐ Brush Teeth
- ☐ Brush Hair
- ☐ Get Backpack Ready
- ☐ Put Shoes On

BEDTIME

- ☐ Clean Room
- ☐ Bath Time
- ☐ Put On Pajamas
- ☐ Brush Teeth
- ☐ Potty Time
- ☐ Read Book
- ☐ Goodnight Kiss

Today Is:____________________

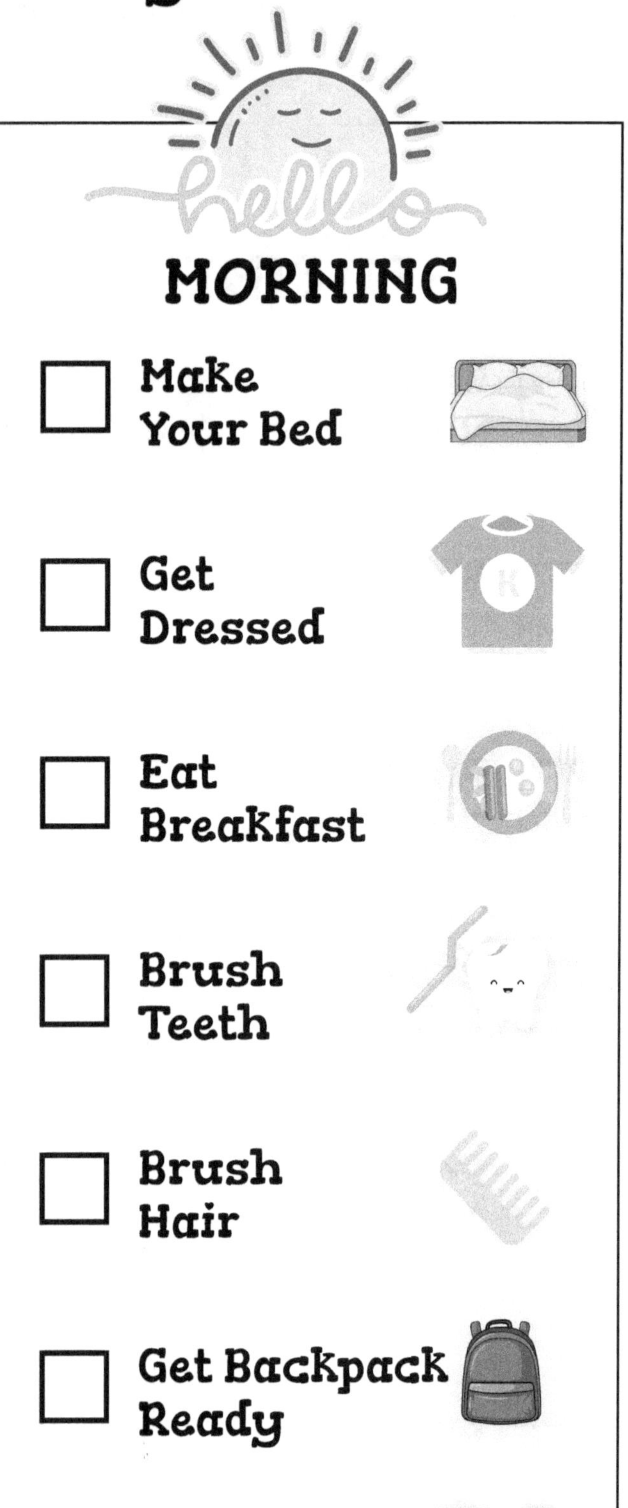

MORNING

- ☐ Make Your Bed
- ☐ Get Dressed
- ☐ Eat Breakfast
- ☐ Brush Teeth
- ☐ Brush Hair
- ☐ Get Backpack Ready
- ☐ Put Shoes On

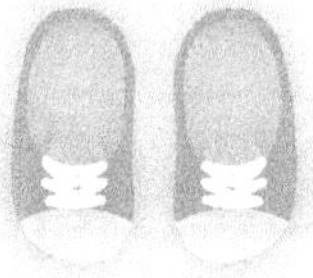

BEDTIME

- ☐ Clean Room 
- ☐ Bath Time 
- ☐ Put On Pajamas 
- ☐ Brush Teeth 
- ☐ Potty Time 
- ☐ Read Book
- ☐ Goodnight Kiss

Today Is:_______________

MORNING

- ☐ Make Your Bed 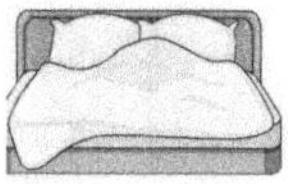
- ☐ Get Dressed 
- ☐ Eat Breakfast 
- ☐ Brush Teeth 
- ☐ Brush Hair 
- ☐ Get Backpack Ready 
- ☐ Put Shoes On

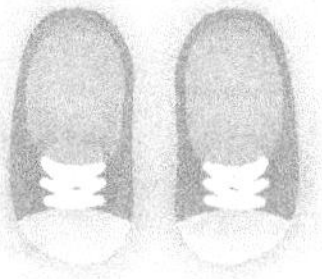

BEDTIME

- ☐ Clean Room 
- ☐ Bath Time 
- ☐ Put On Pajamas 
- ☐ Brush Teeth 
- ☐ Potty Time
- ☐ Read Book 
- ☐ Goodnight Kiss

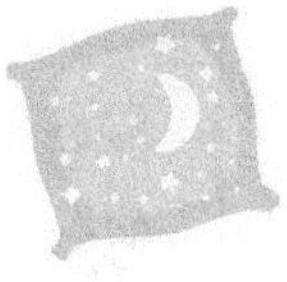

Today Is:_______________________

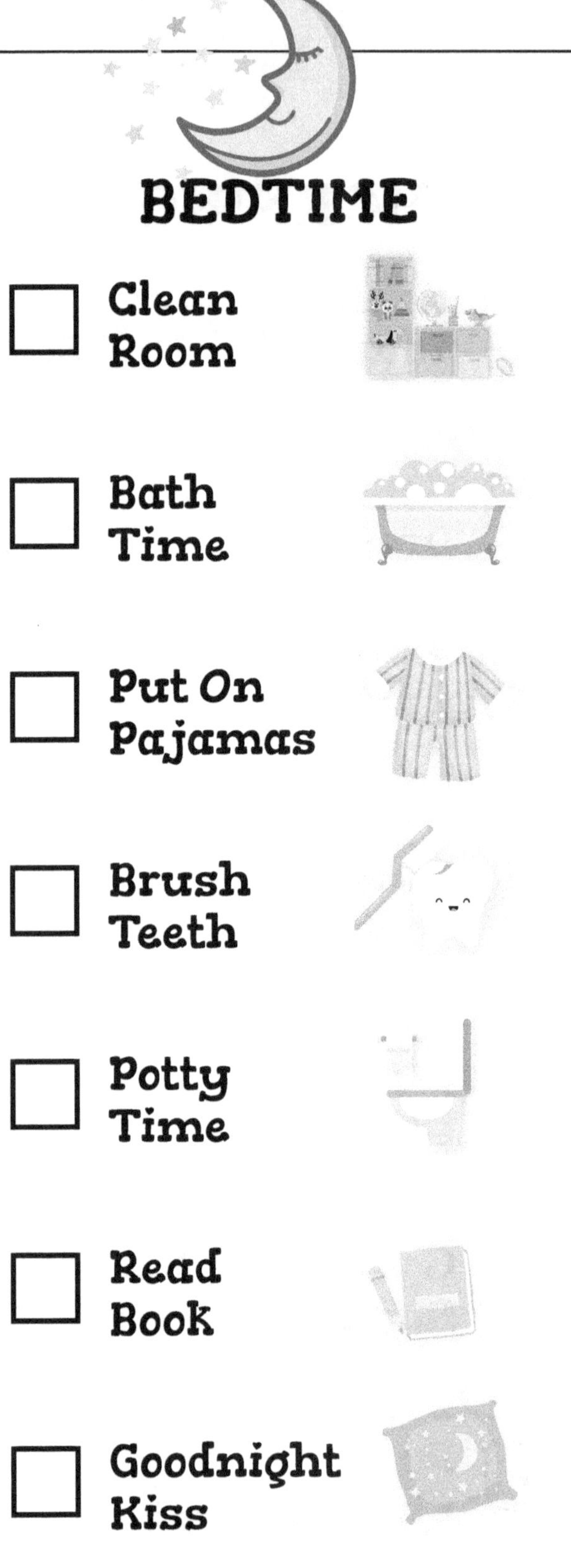

MORNING

- ☐ Make Your Bed 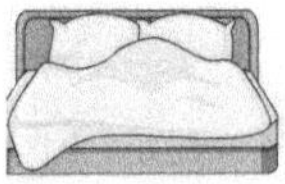
- ☐ Get Dressed 
- ☐ Eat Breakfast 
- ☐ Brush Teeth 
- ☐ Brush Hair
- ☐ Get Backpack Ready 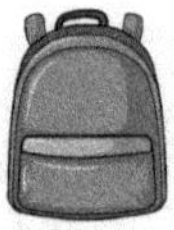
- ☐ Put Shoes On

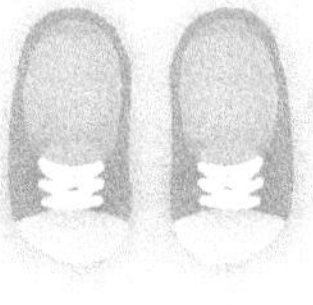

BEDTIME

- ☐ Clean Room
- ☐ Bath Time
- ☐ Put On Pajamas
- ☐ Brush Teeth
- ☐ Potty Time
- ☐ Read Book
- ☐ Goodnight Kiss

Today Is:________________

MORNING

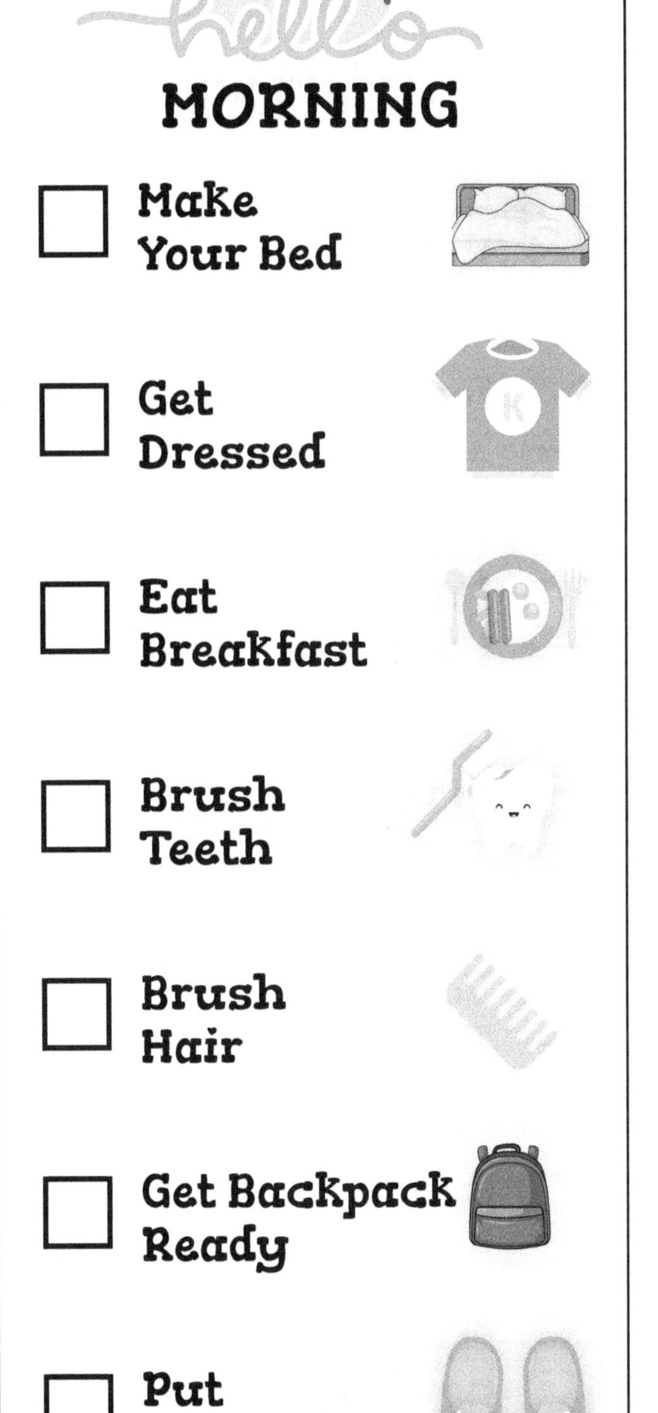

- [ ] Make Your Bed
- [ ] Get Dressed
- [ ] Eat Breakfast
- [ ] Brush Teeth
- [ ] Brush Hair
- [ ] Get Backpack Ready
- [ ] Put Shoes On

BEDTIME

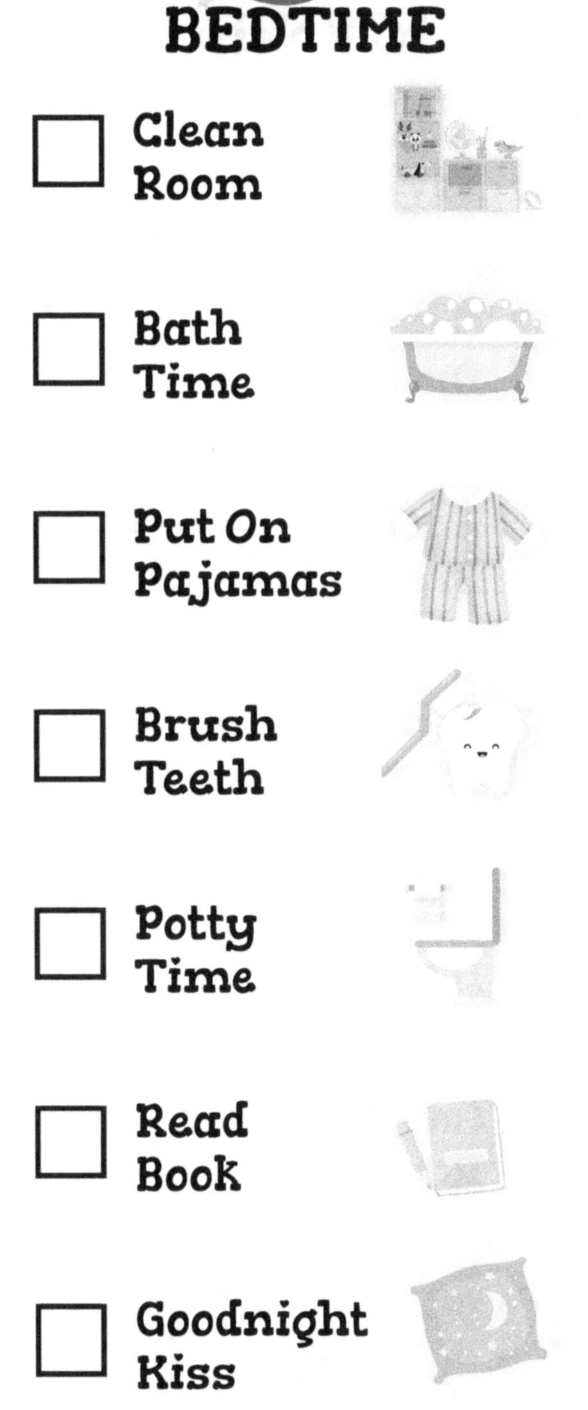

- [ ] Clean Room
- [ ] Bath Time
- [ ] Put On Pajamas
- [ ] Brush Teeth
- [ ] Potty Time
- [ ] Read Book
- [ ] Goodnight Kiss

Today Is:____________________

MORNING

- ☐ Make Your Bed 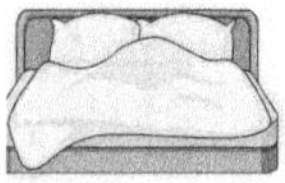
- ☐ Get Dressed 
- ☐ Eat Breakfast 
- ☐ Brush Teeth 
- ☐ Brush Hair
- ☐ Get Backpack Ready 
- ☐ Put Shoes On

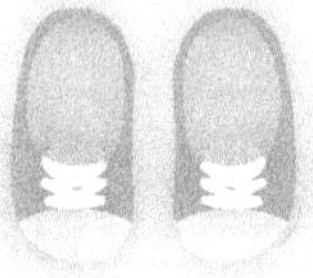

BEDTIME

- ☐ Clean Room 
- ☐ Bath Time 
- ☐ Put On Pajamas 
- ☐ Brush Teeth 
- ☐ Potty Time 
- ☐ Read Book 
- ☐ Goodnight Kiss

Today Is: _______________

MORNING

- ☐ Make Your Bed
- ☐ Get Dressed
- ☐ Eat Breakfast
- ☐ Brush Teeth
- ☐ Brush Hair
- ☐ Get Backpack Ready 
- ☐ Put Shoes On

BEDTIME

- ☐ Clean Room
- ☐ Bath Time
- ☐ Put On Pajamas
- ☐ Brush Teeth
- ☐ Potty Time
- ☐ Read Book
- ☐ Goodnight Kiss

Today Is:_______________

MORNING

- [ ] Make Your Bed 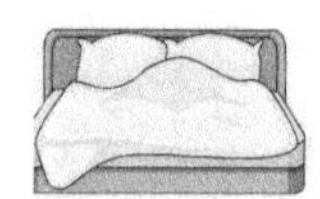
- [ ] Get Dressed 
- [ ] Eat Breakfast 
- [ ] Brush Teeth 
- [ ] Brush Hair 
- [ ] Get Backpack Ready 
- [ ] Put Shoes On 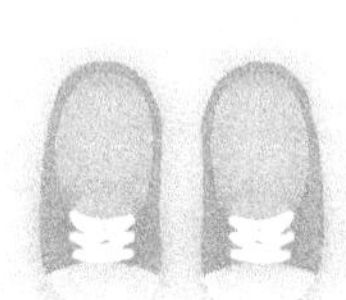

BEDTIME

- [ ] Clean Room 
- [ ] Bath Time 
- [ ] Put On Pajamas 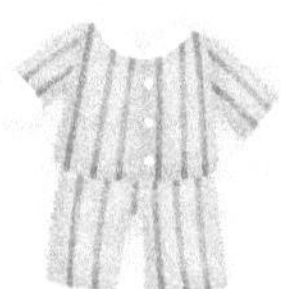
- [ ] Brush Teeth 
- [ ] Potty Time 
- [ ] Read Book 
- [ ] Goodnight Kiss 

Today Is:_______________

MORNING

- ☐ Make Your Bed
- ☐ Get Dressed
- ☐ Eat Breakfast
- ☐ Brush Teeth
- ☐ Brush Hair
- ☐ Get Backpack Ready
- ☐ Put Shoes On

BEDTIME

- ☐ Clean Room
- ☐ Bath Time
- ☐ Put On Pajamas
- ☐ Brush Teeth
- ☐ Potty Time
- ☐ Read Book
- ☐ Goodnight Kiss

Today Is:______________________

MORNING	BEDTIME

MORNING

- ☐ Make Your Bed
- ☐ Get Dressed
- ☐ Eat Breakfast
- ☐ Brush Teeth
- ☐ Brush Hair
- ☐ Get Backpack Ready 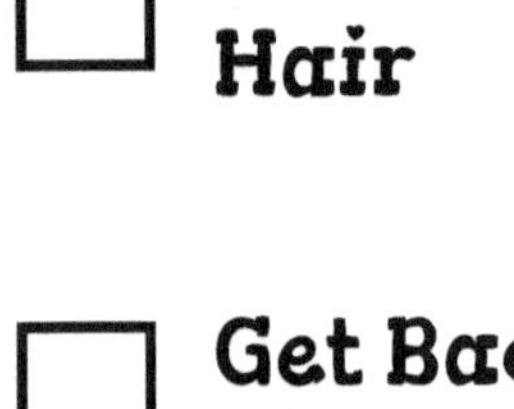
- ☐ Put Shoes On 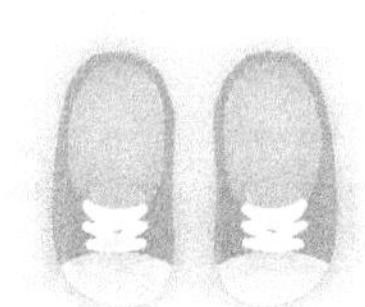

BEDTIME

- ☐ Clean Room 
- ☐ Bath Time 
- ☐ Put On Pajamas
- ☐ Brush Teeth
- ☐ Potty Time
- ☐ Read Book
- ☐ Goodnight Kiss 

Today Is:_______________

MORNING

- ☐ Make Your Bed
- ☐ Get Dressed
- ☐ Eat Breakfast
- ☐ Brush Teeth
- ☐ Brush Hair
- ☐ Get Backpack Ready
- ☐ Put Shoes On

BEDTIME

- ☐ Clean Room
- ☐ Bath Time
- ☐ Put On Pajamas
- ☐ Brush Teeth
- ☐ Potty Time
- ☐ Read Book
- ☐ Goodnight Kiss

Today Is:________________________

MORNING

- ☐ Make Your Bed
- ☐ Get Dressed
- ☐ Eat Breakfast
- ☐ Brush Teeth
- ☐ Brush Hair
- ☐ Get Backpack Ready
- ☐ Put Shoes On

BEDTIME

- ☐ Clean Room
- ☐ Bath Time
- ☐ Put On Pajamas
- ☐ Brush Teeth
- ☐ Potty Time
- ☐ Read Book
- ☐ Goodnight Kiss

Today Is:_______________

MORNING

- ☐ Make Your Bed
- ☐ Get Dressed
- ☐ Eat Breakfast
- ☐ Brush Teeth
- ☐ Brush Hair
- ☐ Get Backpack Ready
- ☐ Put Shoes On

BEDTIME

- ☐ Clean Room
- ☐ Bath Time
- ☐ Put On Pajamas
- ☐ Brush Teeth
- ☐ Potty Time
- ☐ Read Book
- ☐ Goodnight Kiss

MORNING

- [ ] Make Your Bed 
- [ ] Get Dressed 
- [ ] Eat Breakfast 
- [ ] Brush Teeth 
- [ ] Brush Hair 
- [ ] Get Backpack Ready 
- [ ] Put Shoes On 

BEDTIME

- [ ] Clean Room 
- [ ] Bath Time 
- [ ] Put On Pajamas 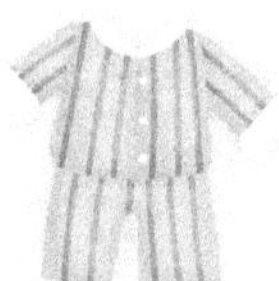
- [ ] Brush Teeth 
- [ ] Potty Time 
- [ ] Read Book 
- [ ] Goodnight Kiss 

Today Is:_______________

MORNING

- ☐ Make Your Bed
- ☐ Get Dressed
- ☐ Eat Breakfast
- ☐ Brush Teeth
- ☐ Brush Hair
- ☐ Get Backpack Ready
- ☐ Put Shoes On

BEDTIME

- ☐ Clean Room
- ☐ Bath Time
- ☐ Put On Pajamas
- ☐ Brush Teeth
- ☐ Potty Time
- ☐ Read Book
- ☐ Goodnight Kiss

Today Is:_______________

MORNING

- ☐ Make Your Bed
- ☐ Get Dressed
- ☐ Eat Breakfast
- ☐ Brush Teeth
- ☐ Brush Hair
- ☐ Get Backpack Ready
- ☐ Put Shoes On

BEDTIME

- ☐ Clean Room
- ☐ Bath Time
- ☐ Put On Pajamas
- ☐ Brush Teeth
- ☐ Potty Time
- ☐ Read Book
- ☐ Goodnight Kiss

MORNING

- ☐ Make Your Bed
- ☐ Get Dressed
- ☐ Eat Breakfast
- ☐ Brush Teeth
- ☐ Brush Hair
- ☐ Get Backpack Ready
- ☐ Put Shoes On

BEDTIME

- ☐ Clean Room
- ☐ Bath Time
- ☐ Put On Pajamas
- ☐ Brush Teeth
- ☐ Potty Time
- ☐ Read Book
- ☐ Goodnight Kiss

MORNING

- [ ] Make Your Bed
- [ ] Get Dressed
- [ ] Eat Breakfast
- [ ] Brush Teeth
- [ ] Brush Hair
- [ ] Get Backpack Ready
- [ ] Put Shoes On

BEDTIME

- [ ] Clean Room
- [ ] Bath Time
- [ ] Put On Pajamas
- [ ] Brush Teeth
- [ ] Potty Time
- [ ] Read Book
- [ ] Goodnight Kiss

Today Is:_______________

MORNING

- ☐ Make Your Bed 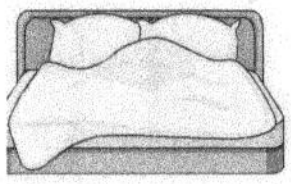
- ☐ Get Dressed 
- ☐ Eat Breakfast 
- ☐ Brush Teeth 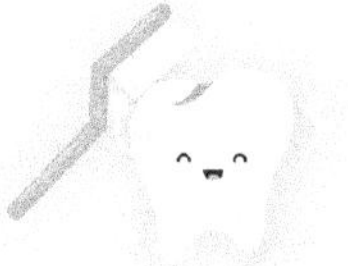
- ☐ Brush Hair
- ☐ Get Backpack Ready 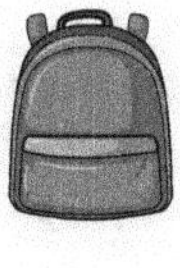
- ☐ Put Shoes On

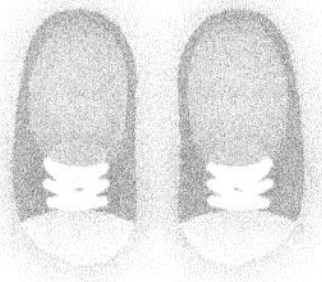

BEDTIME

- ☐ Clean Room 
- ☐ Bath Time 
- ☐ Put On Pajamas 
- ☐ Brush Teeth 
- ☐ Potty Time
- ☐ Read Book
- ☐ Goodnight Kiss

Today Is:___________________

MORNING

- ☐ Make Your Bed 
- ☐ Get Dressed 
- ☐ Eat Breakfast 
- ☐ Brush Teeth 
- ☐ Brush Hair 
- ☐ Get Backpack Ready 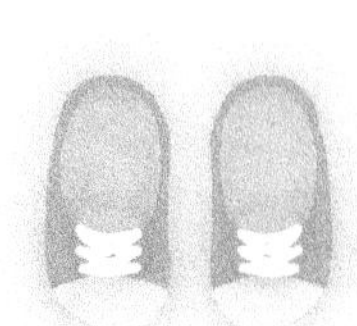
- ☐ Put Shoes On

BEDTIME

- ☐ Clean Room 
- ☐ Bath Time 
- ☐ Put On Pajamas 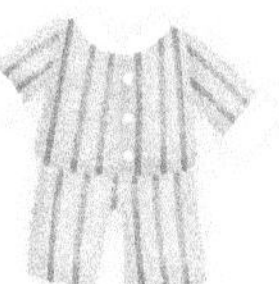
- ☐ Brush Teeth 
- ☐ Potty Time 
- ☐ Read Book 
- ☐ Goodnight Kiss 

Today Is:________

hello

MORNING

☐ Make Your Bed

☐ Get Dressed

☐ Eat Breakfast

☐ Brush Teeth

☐ Brush Hair

☐ Get Backpack Ready

☐ Put Shoes On

BEDTIME

☐ Clean Room

☐ Bath Time

☐ Put On Pajamas

☐ Brush Teeth

☐ Potty Time

☐ Read Book

☐ Goodnight Kiss

Today Is:______________________

MORNING

- ☐ Make Your Bed 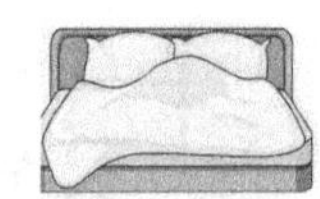
- ☐ Get Dressed 
- ☐ Eat Breakfast 
- ☐ Brush Teeth 
- ☐ Brush Hair 
- ☐ Get Backpack Ready 
- ☐ Put Shoes On 

BEDTIME

- ☐ Clean Room 
- ☐ Bath Time 
- ☐ Put On Pajamas 
- ☐ Brush Teeth 
- ☐ Potty Time 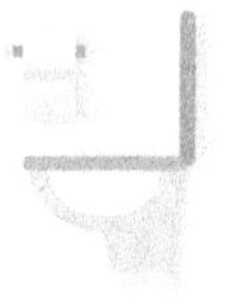
- ☐ Read Book 
- ☐ Goodnight Kiss 

Today Is:________________

MORNING

- ☐ Make Your Bed
- ☐ Get Dressed
- ☐ Eat Breakfast
- ☐ Brush Teeth
- ☐ Brush Hair
- ☐ Get Backpack Ready
- ☐ Put Shoes On

BEDTIME

- ☐ Clean Room
- ☐ Bath Time
- ☐ Put On Pajamas
- ☐ Brush Teeth
- ☐ Potty Time
- ☐ Read Book
- ☐ Goodnight Kiss

Today Is:_______________

<table>
<tr><td>

MORNING

☐ Make Your Bed

☐ Get Dressed

☐ Eat Breakfast

☐ Brush Teeth

☐ Brush Hair

☐ Get Backpack Ready

☐ Put Shoes On

</td><td>

BEDTIME

☐ Clean Room

☐ Bath Time

☐ Put On Pajamas

☐ Brush Teeth

☐ Potty Time

☐ Read Book

☐ Goodnight Kiss

</td></tr>
</table>

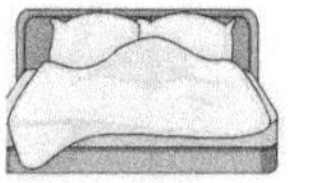

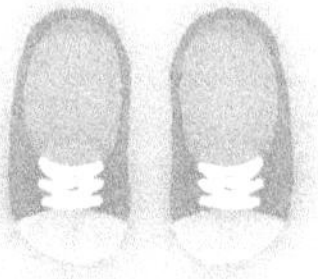

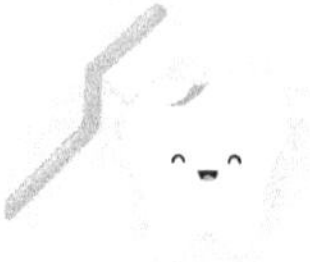

Today Is:_______________

MORNING

- ☐ Make Your Bed
- ☐ Get Dressed
- ☐ Eat Breakfast
- ☐ Brush Teeth
- ☐ Brush Hair
- ☐ Get Backpack Ready
- ☐ Put Shoes On

BEDTIME

- ☐ Clean Room
- ☐ Bath Time
- ☐ Put On Pajamas
- ☐ Brush Teeth
- ☐ Potty Time
- ☐ Read Book
- ☐ Goodnight Kiss

Today Is:_______________________

MORNING

- ☐ Make Your Bed
- ☐ Get Dressed
- ☐ Eat Breakfast
- ☐ Brush Teeth
- ☐ Brush Hair
- ☐ Get Backpack Ready
- ☐ Put Shoes On

BEDTIME

- ☐ Clean Room
- ☐ Bath Time
- ☐ Put On Pajamas
- ☐ Brush Teeth
- ☐ Potty Time
- ☐ Read Book
- ☐ Goodnight Kiss

Today Is:_______________

MORNING

- ☐ Make Your Bed
- ☐ Get Dressed
- ☐ Eat Breakfast
- ☐ Brush Teeth
- ☐ Brush Hair
- ☐ Get Backpack Ready
- ☐ Put Shoes On

BEDTIME

- ☐ Clean Room
- ☐ Bath Time
- ☐ Put On Pajamas
- ☐ Brush Teeth
- ☐ Potty Time
- ☐ Read Book
- ☐ Goodnight Kiss

Today Is:_______________

MORNING

- ☐ Make Your Bed 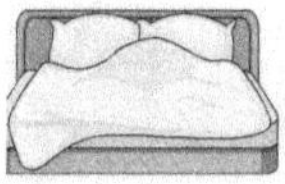
- ☐ Get Dressed 
- ☐ Eat Breakfast 
- ☐ Brush Teeth 
- ☐ Brush Hair
- ☐ Get Backpack Ready 
- ☐ Put Shoes On

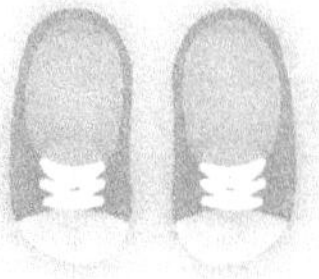

BEDTIME

- ☐ Clean Room 
- ☐ Bath Time 
- ☐ Put On Pajamas 
- ☐ Brush Teeth 
- ☐ Potty Time
- ☐ Read Book
- ☐ Goodnight Kiss

Today Is:_______________

MORNING

- [ ] Make Your Bed 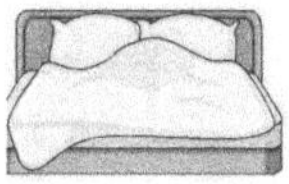
- [ ] Get Dressed 
- [ ] Eat Breakfast 
- [ ] Brush Teeth 
- [ ] Brush Hair
- [ ] Get Backpack Ready 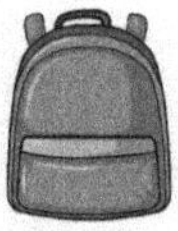
- [ ] Put Shoes On

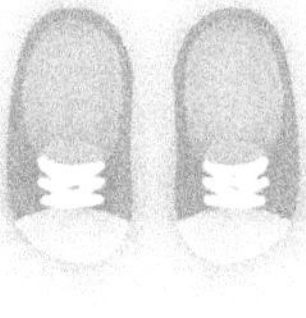

BEDTIME

- [ ] Clean Room 
- [ ] Bath Time 
- [ ] Put On Pajamas 
- [ ] Brush Teeth 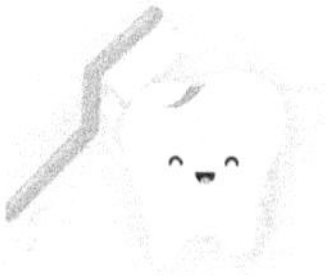
- [ ] Potty Time
- [ ] Read Book
- [ ] Goodnight Kiss

Today Is: ____________________

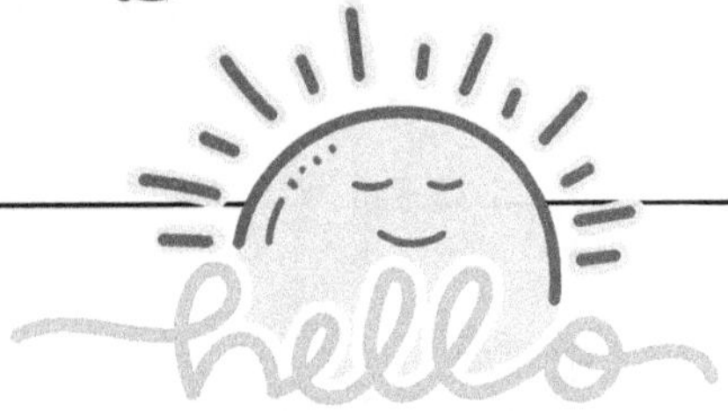

MORNING

- [ ] Make Your Bed 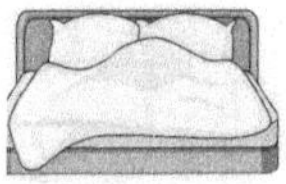
- [ ] Get Dressed 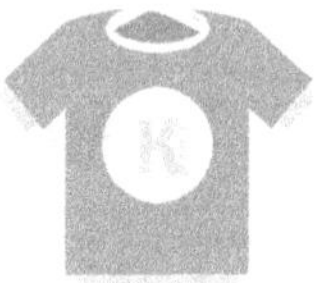
- [ ] Eat Breakfast 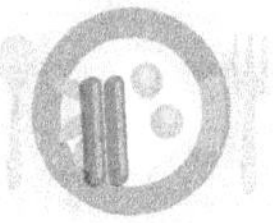
- [ ] Brush Teeth 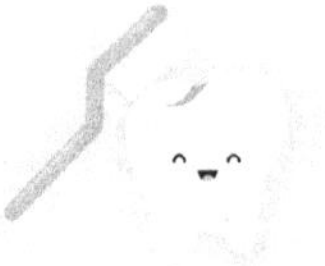
- [ ] Brush Hair
- [ ] Get Backpack Ready
- [ ] Put Shoes On

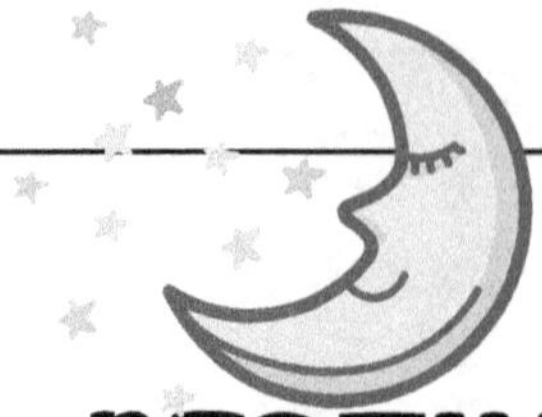

BEDTIME

- [ ] Clean Room 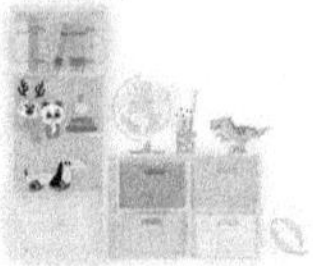
- [ ] Bath Time 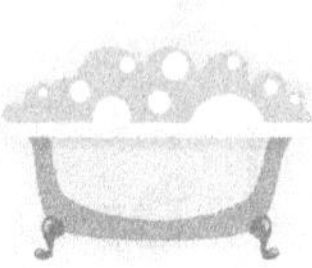
- [ ] Put On Pajamas 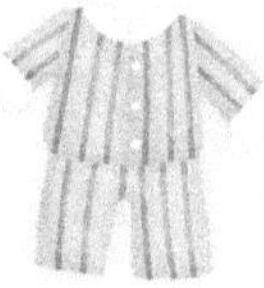
- [ ] Brush Teeth 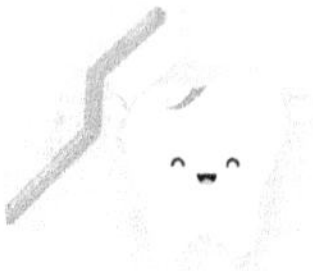
- [ ] Potty Time
- [ ] Read Book
- [ ] Goodnight Kiss

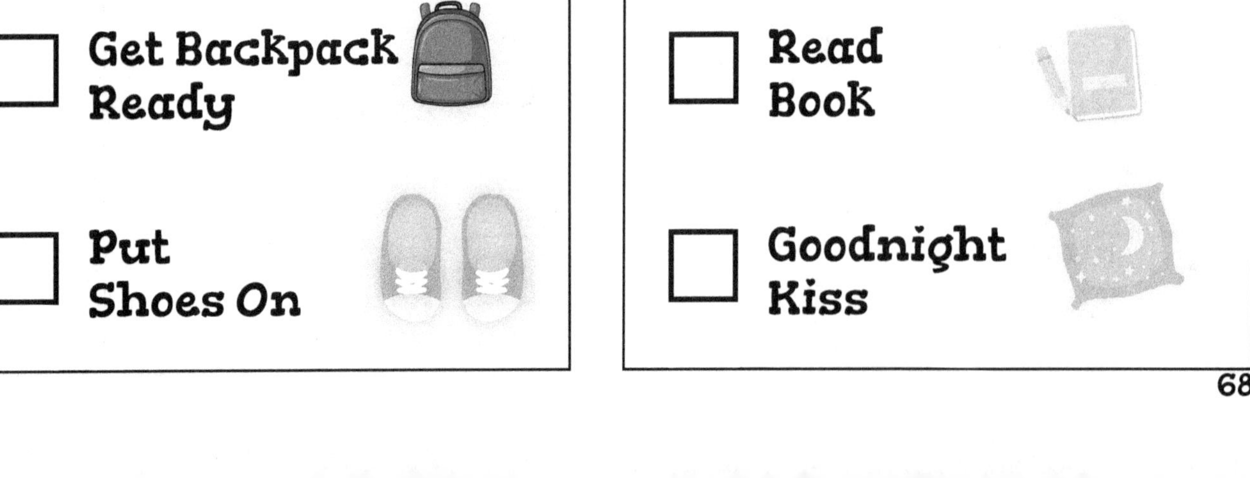

Today Is:_______________________

MORNING

- ☐ Make Your Bed
- ☐ Get Dressed
- ☐ Eat Breakfast
- ☐ Brush Teeth
- ☐ Brush Hair
- ☐ Get Backpack Ready
- ☐ Put Shoes On

BEDTIME

- ☐ Clean Room
- ☐ Bath Time
- ☐ Put On Pajamas
- ☐ Brush Teeth
- ☐ Potty Time
- ☐ Read Book
- ☐ Goodnight Kiss

Today Is: ____________________

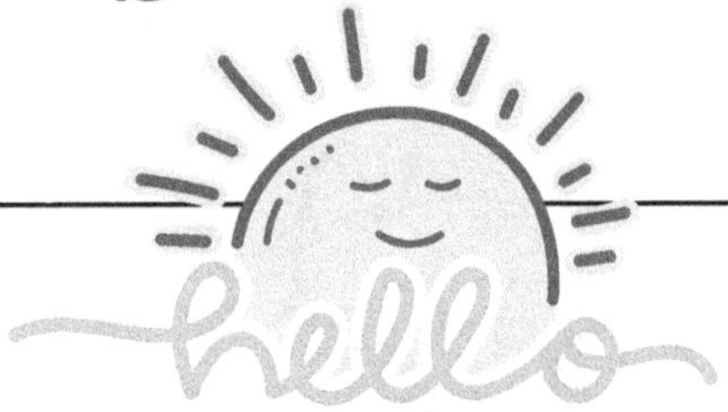

MORNING

☐ Make Your Bed 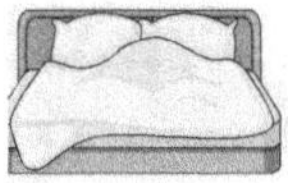

☐ Get Dressed 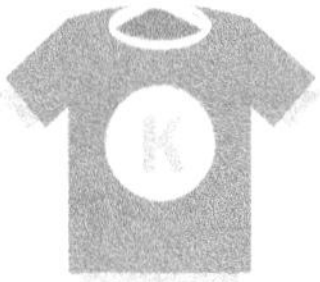

☐ Eat Breakfast 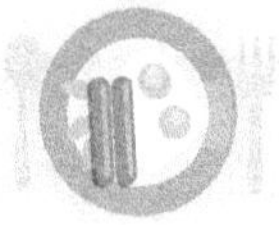

☐ Brush Teeth 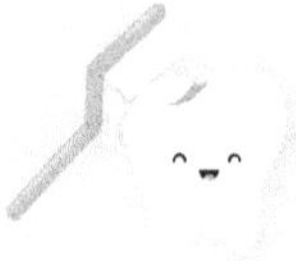

☐ Brush Hair

☐ Get Backpack Ready 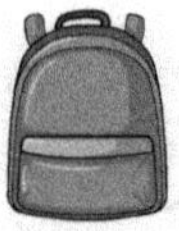

☐ Put Shoes On 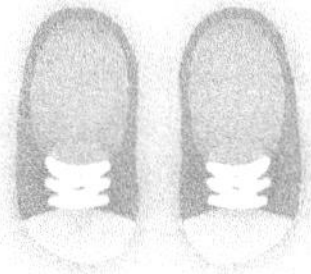

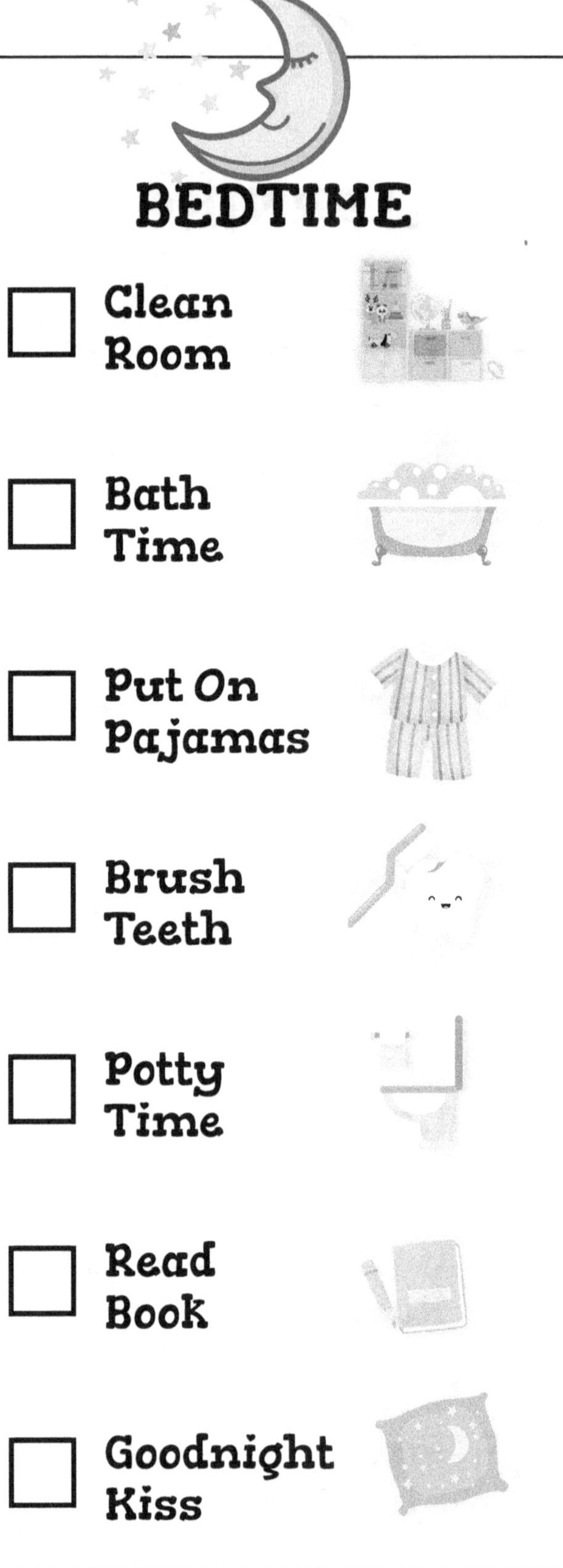

BEDTIME

☐ Clean Room

☐ Bath Time

☐ Put On Pajamas

☐ Brush Teeth

☐ Potty Time

☐ Read Book

☐ Goodnight Kiss

Today Is:_______________

MORNING

- ☐ Make Your Bed
- ☐ Get Dressed
- ☐ Eat Breakfast
- ☐ Brush Teeth
- ☐ Brush Hair
- ☐ Get Backpack Ready
- ☐ Put Shoes On

BEDTIME

- ☐ Clean Room
- ☐ Bath Time
- ☐ Put On Pajamas
- ☐ Brush Teeth
- ☐ Potty Time
- ☐ Read Book
- ☐ Goodnight Kiss

Today Is:______________________

MORNING

- ☐ Make Your Bed 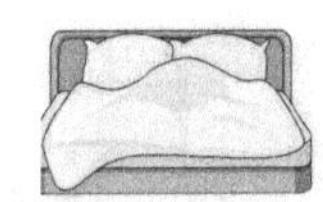
- ☐ Get Dressed 
- ☐ Eat Breakfast 
- ☐ Brush Teeth 
- ☐ Brush Hair 
- ☐ Get Backpack Ready 
- ☐ Put Shoes On 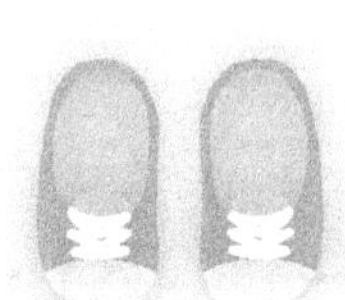

BEDTIME

- ☐ Clean Room 
- ☐ Bath Time 
- ☐ Put On Pajamas 
- ☐ Brush Teeth 
- ☐ Potty Time 
- ☐ Read Book 
- ☐ Goodnight Kiss 

Today Is:_______________

MORNING

- ☐ Make Your Bed
- ☐ Get Dressed
- ☐ Eat Breakfast
- ☐ Brush Teeth
- ☐ Brush Hair
- ☐ Get Backpack Ready
- ☐ Put Shoes On

BEDTIME

- ☐ Clean Room
- ☐ Bath Time
- ☐ Put On Pajamas
- ☐ Brush Teeth
- ☐ Potty Time
- ☐ Read Book
- ☐ Goodnight Kiss

Today Is:___________________

MORNING

- ☐ Make Your Bed 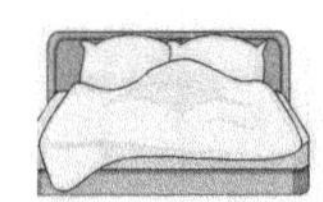
- ☐ Get Dressed 
- ☐ Eat Breakfast 
- ☐ Brush Teeth 
- ☐ Brush Hair 
- ☐ Get Backpack Ready 
- ☐ Put Shoes On 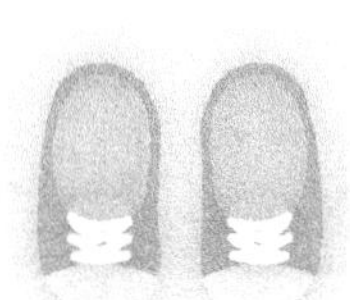

BEDTIME

- ☐ Clean Room 
- ☐ Bath Time 
- ☐ Put On Pajamas 
- ☐ Brush Teeth 
- ☐ Potty Time 
- ☐ Read Book 
- ☐ Goodnight Kiss 

Today Is:_______________

MORNING

- ☐ Make Your Bed
- ☐ Get Dressed
- ☐ Eat Breakfast
- ☐ Brush Teeth
- ☐ Brush Hair
- ☐ Get Backpack Ready
- ☐ Put Shoes On

BEDTIME

- ☐ Clean Room
- ☐ Bath Time
- ☐ Put On Pajamas
- ☐ Brush Teeth
- ☐ Potty Time
- ☐ Read Book
- ☐ Goodnight Kiss

Today Is:_______________

MORNING

- ☐ Make Your Bed
- ☐ Get Dressed
- ☐ Eat Breakfast
- ☐ Brush Teeth
- ☐ Brush Hair
- ☐ Get Backpack Ready
- ☐ Put Shoes On

BEDTIME

- ☐ Clean Room
- ☐ Bath Time
- ☐ Put On Pajamas
- ☐ Brush Teeth
- ☐ Potty Time
- ☐ Read Book
- ☐ Goodnight Kiss

Today Is:_______________

MORNING

- ☐ Make Your Bed
- ☐ Get Dressed
- ☐ Eat Breakfast
- ☐ Brush Teeth
- ☐ Brush Hair
- ☐ Get Backpack Ready
- ☐ Put Shoes On

BEDTIME

- ☐ Clean Room
- ☐ Bath Time
- ☐ Put On Pajamas
- ☐ Brush Teeth
- ☐ Potty Time
- ☐ Read Book
- ☐ Goodnight Kiss

Today Is: ____________________

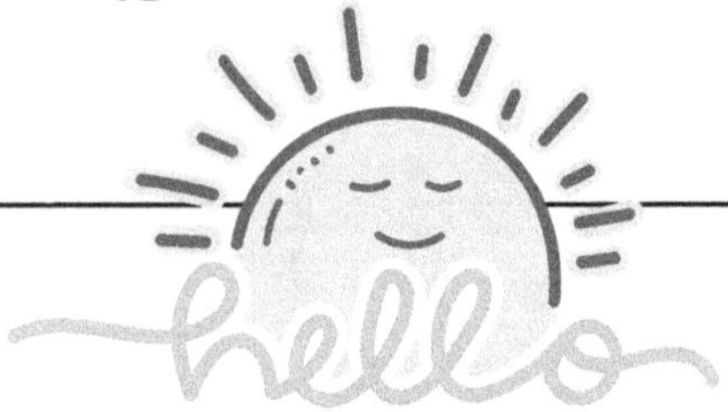

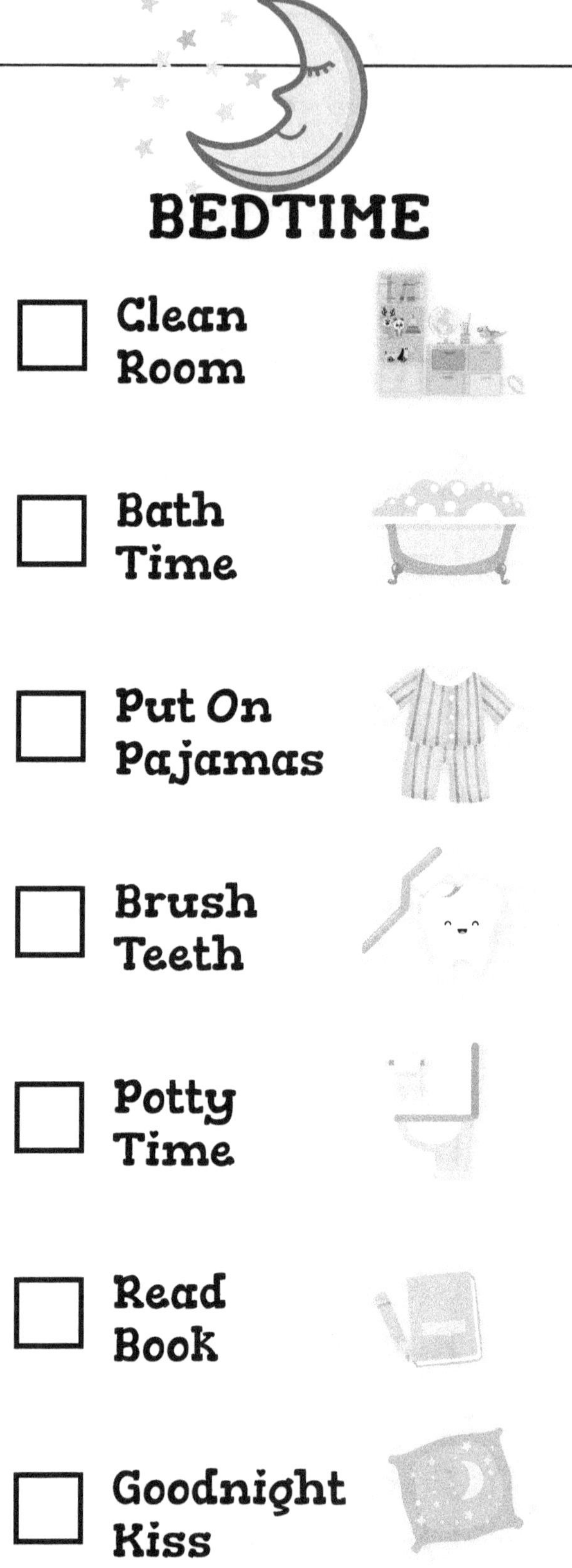

MORNING

- ☐ Make Your Bed
- ☐ Get Dressed
- ☐ Eat Breakfast
- ☐ Brush Teeth
- ☐ Brush Hair
- ☐ Get Backpack Ready
- ☐ Put Shoes On

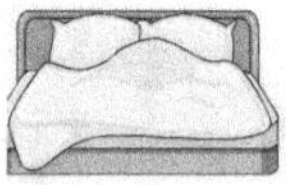

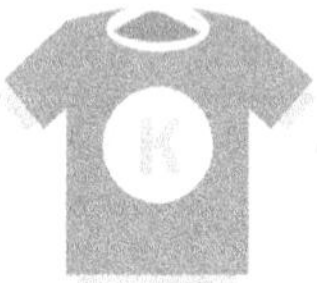

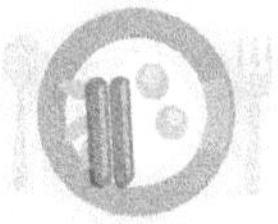

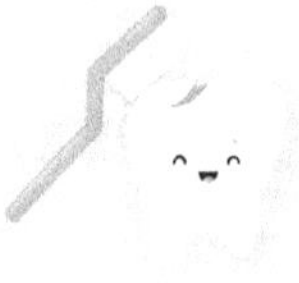

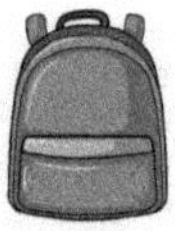

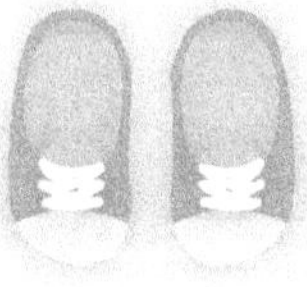

BEDTIME

- ☐ Clean Room
- ☐ Bath Time
- ☐ Put On Pajamas
- ☐ Brush Teeth
- ☐ Potty Time
- ☐ Read Book
- ☐ Goodnight Kiss

Today Is:________________________

MORNING

- ☐ Make Your Bed 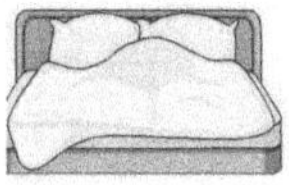
- ☐ Get Dressed 
- ☐ Eat Breakfast 
- ☐ Brush Teeth 
- ☐ Brush Hair
- ☐ Get Backpack Ready 
- ☐ Put Shoes On

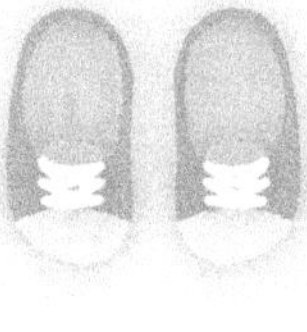

BEDTIME

- ☐ Clean Room 
- ☐ Bath Time 
- ☐ Put On Pajamas 
- ☐ Brush Teeth 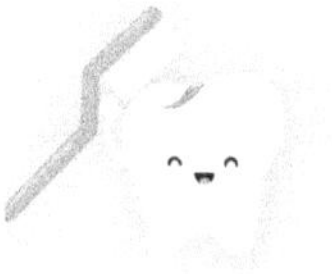
- ☐ Potty Time
- ☐ Read Book
- ☐ Goodnight Kiss

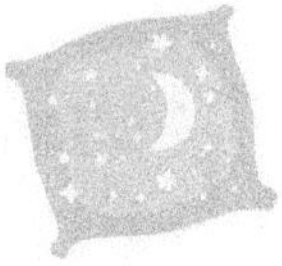

Today Is:_______________

MORNING

- ☐ Make Your Bed 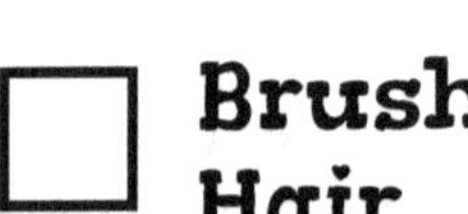
- ☐ Get Dressed 
- ☐ Eat Breakfast 
- ☐ Brush Teeth
- ☐ Brush Hair
- ☐ Get Backpack Ready 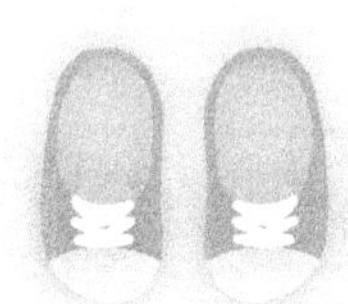
- ☐ Put Shoes On

BEDTIME

- ☐ Clean Room 
- ☐ Bath Time 
- ☐ Put On Pajamas
- ☐ Brush Teeth 
- ☐ Potty Time
- ☐ Read Book 
- ☐ Goodnight Kiss 

Today Is:______________________

MORNING

- ☐ Make Your Bed
- ☐ Get Dressed
- ☐ Eat Breakfast
- ☐ Brush Teeth
- ☐ Brush Hair
- ☐ Get Backpack Ready
- ☐ Put Shoes On

BEDTIME

- ☐ Clean Room
- ☐ Bath Time
- ☐ Put On Pajamas
- ☐ Brush Teeth
- ☐ Potty Time
- ☐ Read Book
- ☐ Goodnight Kiss

Today Is:_______________

MORNING

- ☐ Make Your Bed 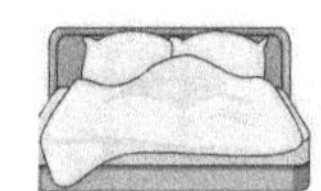
- ☐ Get Dressed 
- ☐ Eat Breakfast 
- ☐ Brush Teeth 
- ☐ Brush Hair 
- ☐ Get Backpack Ready 
- ☐ Put Shoes On 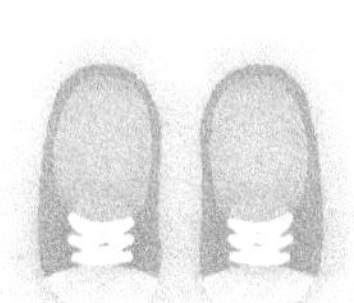

BEDTIME

- ☐ Clean Room 
- ☐ Bath Time 
- ☐ Put On Pajamas 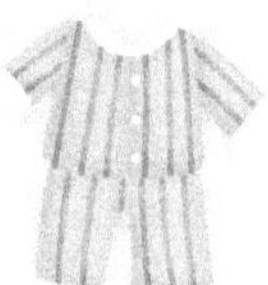
- ☐ Brush Teeth 
- ☐ Potty Time 
- ☐ Read Book 
- ☐ Goodnight Kiss 

Today Is:________________________

MORNING

- [ ] Make Your Bed
- [ ] Get Dressed
- [ ] Eat Breakfast
- [ ] Brush Teeth
- [ ] Brush Hair
- [ ] Get Backpack Ready
- [ ] Put Shoes On

BEDTIME

- [ ] Clean Room
- [ ] Bath Time
- [ ] Put On Pajamas
- [ ] Brush Teeth
- [ ] Potty Time
- [ ] Read Book
- [ ] Goodnight Kiss

Today Is:________________

MORNING

- ☐ Make Your Bed
- ☐ Get Dressed
- ☐ Eat Breakfast
- ☐ Brush Teeth
- ☐ Brush Hair
- ☐ Get Backpack Ready
- ☐ Put Shoes On

BEDTIME

- ☐ Clean Room
- ☐ Bath Time
- ☐ Put On Pajamas
- ☐ Brush Teeth
- ☐ Potty Time
- ☐ Read Book
- ☐ Goodnight Kiss

Today Is:______________

MORNING

- ☐ Make Your Bed
- ☐ Get Dressed
- ☐ Eat Breakfast
- ☐ Brush Teeth
- ☐ Brush Hair
- ☐ Get Backpack Ready
- ☐ Put Shoes On

BEDTIME

- ☐ Clean Room
- ☐ Bath Time
- ☐ Put On Pajamas
- ☐ Brush Teeth
- ☐ Potty Time
- ☐ Read Book
- ☐ Goodnight Kiss

Today Is:_______________

<table>
<tr><td>

MORNING

☐ Make Your Bed 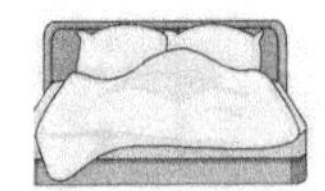

☐ Get Dressed 

☐ Eat Breakfast 

☐ Brush Teeth 

☐ Brush Hair 

☐ Get Backpack Ready 

☐ Put Shoes On 

</td><td>

BEDTIME

☐ Clean Room 

☐ Bath Time 

☐ Put On Pajamas 

☐ Brush Teeth 

☐ Potty Time 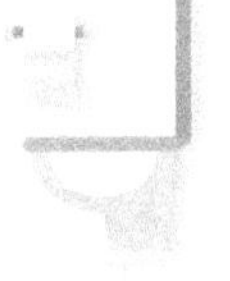

☐ Read Book 

☐ Goodnight Kiss 

</td></tr>
</table>

Today Is:________________

MORNING

- ☐ Make Your Bed
- ☐ Get Dressed
- ☐ Eat Breakfast
- ☐ Brush Teeth
- ☐ Brush Hair
- ☐ Get Backpack Ready
- ☐ Put Shoes On

BEDTIME

- ☐ Clean Room
- ☐ Bath Time
- ☐ Put On Pajamas
- ☐ Brush Teeth
- ☐ Potty Time
- ☐ Read Book
- ☐ Goodnight Kiss

Today Is:_________________

MORNING

- [ ] Make Your Bed
- [ ] Get Dressed
- [ ] Eat Breakfast
- [ ] Brush Teeth
- [ ] Brush Hair
- [ ] Get Backpack Ready 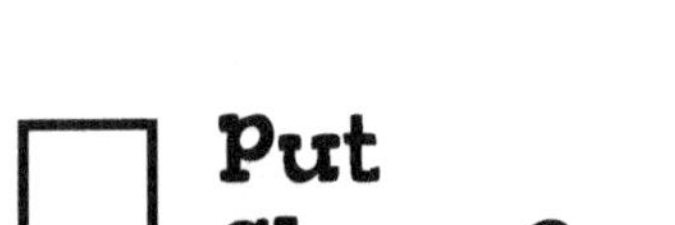
- [ ] Put Shoes On 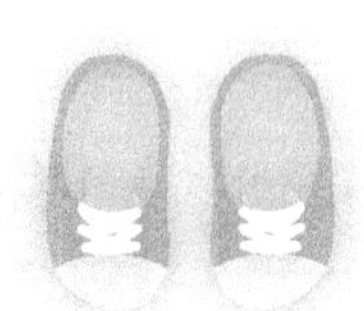

BEDTIME

- [ ] Clean Room
- [ ] Bath Time
- [ ] Put On Pajamas
- [ ] Brush Teeth
- [ ] Potty Time
- [ ] Read Book
- [ ] Goodnight Kiss 

Today Is:________________

MORNING

- ☐ Make Your Bed
- ☐ Get Dressed
- ☐ Eat Breakfast
- ☐ Brush Teeth
- ☐ Brush Hair
- ☐ Get Backpack Ready
- ☐ Put Shoes On

BEDTIME

- ☐ Clean Room
- ☐ Bath Time
- ☐ Put On Pajamas
- ☐ Brush Teeth
- ☐ Potty Time
- ☐ Read Book
- ☐ Goodnight Kiss

Today Is:_______________

MORNING

- [ ] Make Your Bed
- [ ] Get Dressed
- [ ] Eat Breakfast
- [ ] Brush Teeth
- [ ] Brush Hair
- [ ] Get Backpack Ready
- [ ] Put Shoes On

BEDTIME

- [ ] Clean Room
- [ ] Bath Time
- [ ] Put On Pajamas
- [ ] Brush Teeth
- [ ] Potty Time
- [ ] Read Book
- [ ] Goodnight Kiss

Today Is:_______________

MORNING

- ☐ Make Your Bed
- ☐ Get Dressed
- ☐ Eat Breakfast
- ☐ Brush Teeth
- ☐ Brush Hair
- ☐ Get Backpack Ready
- ☐ Put Shoes On

BEDTIME

- ☐ Clean Room
- ☐ Bath Time
- ☐ Put On Pajamas
- ☐ Brush Teeth
- ☐ Potty Time
- ☐ Read Book
- ☐ Goodnight Kiss

Today Is:_______________

MORNING

- ☐ Make Your Bed
- ☐ Get Dressed
- ☐ Eat Breakfast
- ☐ Brush Teeth
- ☐ Brush Hair
- ☐ Get Backpack Ready
- ☐ Put Shoes On

BEDTIME

- ☐ Clean Room
- ☐ Bath Time
- ☐ Put On Pajamas
- ☐ Brush Teeth
- ☐ Potty Time
- ☐ Read Book
- ☐ Goodnight Kiss

Today Is:______________________

MORNING

- [ ] Make Your Bed 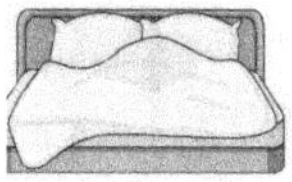
- [ ] Get Dressed 
- [ ] Eat Breakfast 
- [ ] Brush Teeth 
- [ ] Brush Hair
- [ ] Get Backpack Ready 
- [ ] Put Shoes On

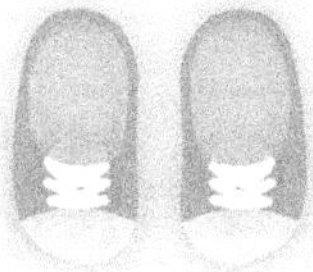

BEDTIME

- [ ] Clean Room 
- [ ] Bath Time 
- [ ] Put On Pajamas 
- [ ] Brush Teeth 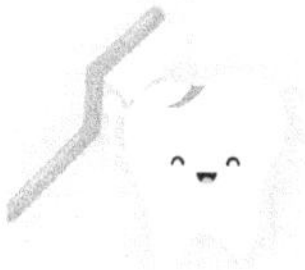
- [ ] Potty Time
- [ ] Read Book
- [ ] Goodnight Kiss

Today Is:_____________

MORNING

- ☐ Make Your Bed
- ☐ Get Dressed
- ☐ Eat Breakfast
- ☐ Brush Teeth
- ☐ Brush Hair
- ☐ Get Backpack Ready
- ☐ Put Shoes On

BEDTIME

- ☐ Clean Room
- ☐ Bath Time
- ☐ Put On Pajamas
- ☐ Brush Teeth
- ☐ Potty Time
- ☐ Read Book
- ☐ Goodnight Kiss

MORNING

- ☐ Make Your Bed 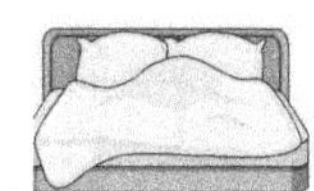
- ☐ Get Dressed 
- ☐ Eat Breakfast 
- ☐ Brush Teeth 
- ☐ Brush Hair 
- ☐ Get Backpack Ready 
- ☐ Put Shoes On 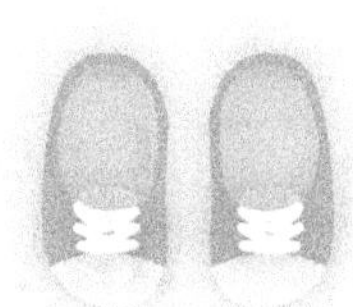

BEDTIME

- ☐ Clean Room 
- ☐ Bath Time 
- ☐ Put On Pajamas 
- ☐ Brush Teeth 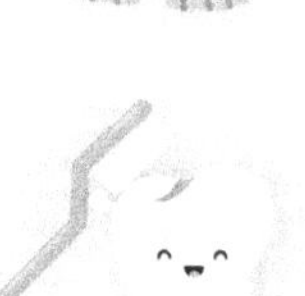
- ☐ Potty Time 
- ☐ Read Book 
- ☐ Goodnight Kiss 

Today Is:_______________

<table>
<tr><td>

MORNING

☐ Make Your Bed

☐ Get Dressed

☐ Eat Breakfast

☐ Brush Teeth

☐ Brush Hair

☐ Get Backpack Ready

☐ Put Shoes On

</td><td>

BEDTIME

☐ Clean Room

☐ Bath Time

☐ Put On Pajamas

☐ Brush Teeth

☐ Potty Time

☐ Read Book

☐ Goodnight Kiss

</td></tr>
</table>

Today Is: __________________

MORNING

- ☐ Make Your Bed
- ☐ Get Dressed
- ☐ Eat Breakfast
- ☐ Brush Teeth
- ☐ Brush Hair
- ☐ Get Backpack Ready 
- ☐ Put Shoes On 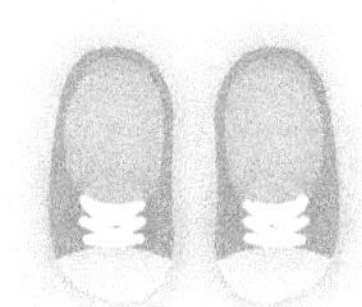

BEDTIME

- ☐ Clean Room
- ☐ Bath Time
- ☐ Put On Pajamas
- ☐ Brush Teeth
- ☐ Potty Time
- ☐ Read Book 
- ☐ Goodnight Kiss 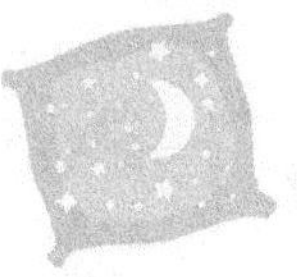

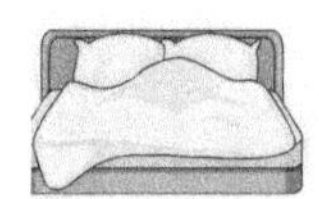

MORNING

- ☐ Make Your Bed 
- ☐ Get Dressed 
- ☐ Eat Breakfast 
- ☐ Brush Teeth 
- ☐ Brush Hair 
- ☐ Get Backpack Ready 
- ☐ Put Shoes On 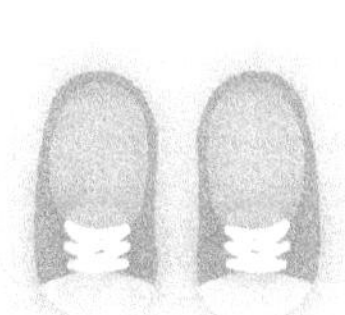

BEDTIME

- ☐ Clean Room 
- ☐ Bath Time 
- ☐ Put On Pajamas 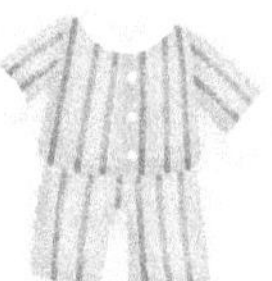
- ☐ Brush Teeth 
- ☐ Potty Time 
- ☐ Read Book 
- ☐ Goodnight Kiss 

Today Is:_______________

MORNING

- ☐ Make Your Bed
- ☐ Get Dressed
- ☐ Eat Breakfast
- ☐ Brush Teeth
- ☐ Brush Hair
- ☐ Get Backpack Ready
- ☐ Put Shoes On

BEDTIME

- ☐ Clean Room
- ☐ Bath Time
- ☐ Put On Pajamas
- ☐ Brush Teeth
- ☐ Potty Time
- ☐ Read Book
- ☐ Goodnight Kiss

Today Is:_______________________

MORNING

- ☐ Make Your Bed
- ☐ Get Dressed
- ☐ Eat Breakfast
- ☐ Brush Teeth
- ☐ Brush Hair
- ☐ Get Backpack Ready
- ☐ Put Shoes On

BEDTIME

- ☐ Clean Room
- ☐ Bath Time
- ☐ Put On Pajamas
- ☐ Brush Teeth
- ☐ Potty Time
- ☐ Read Book
- ☐ Goodnight Kiss

Today Is:______________________

MORNING

- ☐ Make Your Bed 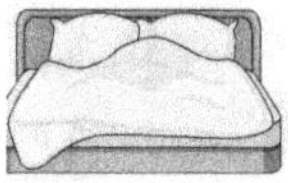
- ☐ Get Dressed 
- ☐ Eat Breakfast 
- ☐ Brush Teeth 
- ☐ Brush Hair
- ☐ Get Backpack Ready 
- ☐ Put Shoes On

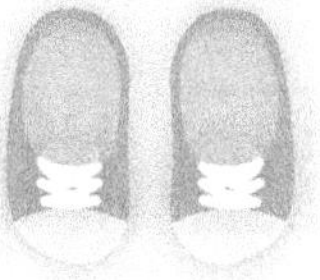

BEDTIME

- ☐ Clean Room 
- ☐ Bath Time 
- ☐ Put On Pajamas 
- ☐ Brush Teeth 
- ☐ Potty Time
- ☐ Read Book 
- ☐ Goodnight Kiss

Today Is:________________

MORNING

- ☐ Make Your Bed
- ☐ Get Dressed
- ☐ Eat Breakfast
- ☐ Brush Teeth
- ☐ Brush Hair
- ☐ Get Backpack Ready
- ☐ Put Shoes On

BEDTIME

- ☐ Clean Room
- ☐ Bath Time
- ☐ Put On Pajamas
- ☐ Brush Teeth
- ☐ Potty Time
- ☐ Read Book
- ☐ Goodnight Kiss

Today Is: _______________

MORNING

- ☐ Make Your Bed 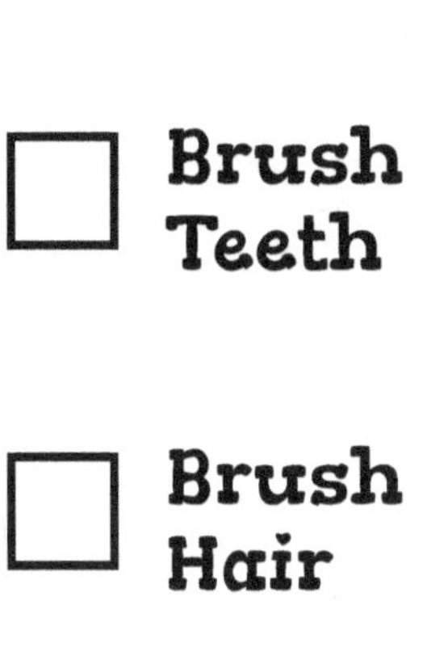
- ☐ Get Dressed
- ☐ Eat Breakfast
- ☐ Brush Teeth
- ☐ Brush Hair
- ☐ Get Backpack Ready 
- ☐ Put Shoes On 

BEDTIME

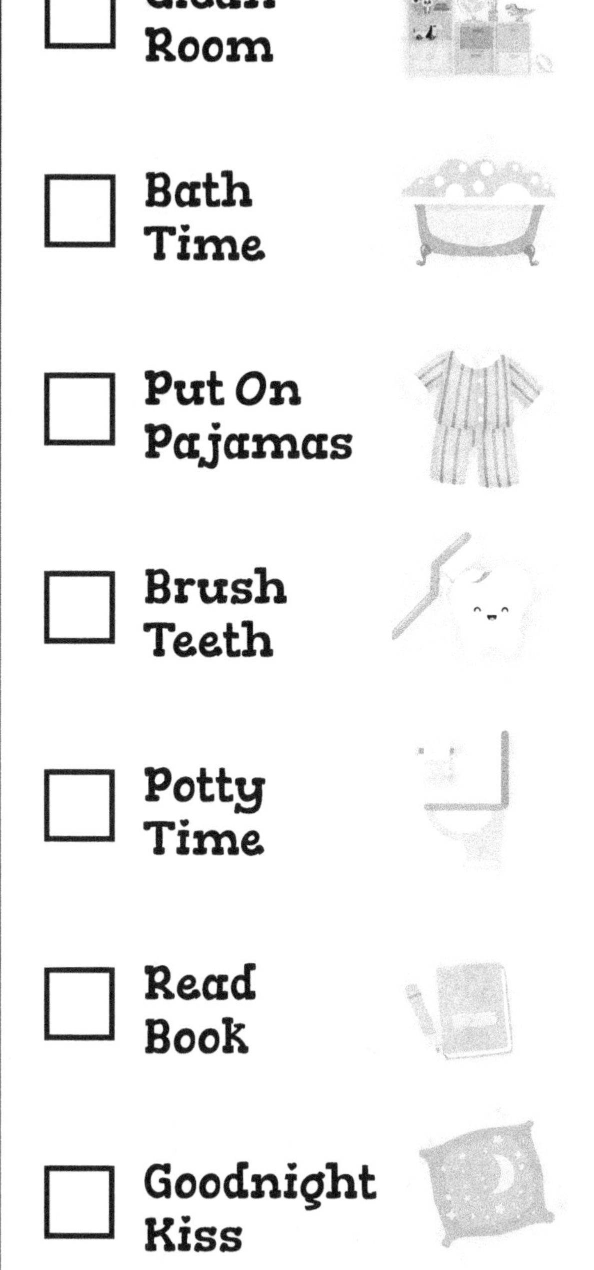

- ☐ Clean Room
- ☐ Bath Time
- ☐ Put On Pajamas
- ☐ Brush Teeth
- ☐ Potty Time
- ☐ Read Book
- ☐ Goodnight Kiss

Today Is:________________

MORNING

- [ ] Make Your Bed 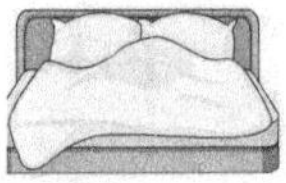
- [ ] Get Dressed 
- [ ] Eat Breakfast 
- [ ] Brush Teeth 
- [ ] Brush Hair
- [ ] Get Backpack Ready 
- [ ] Put Shoes On

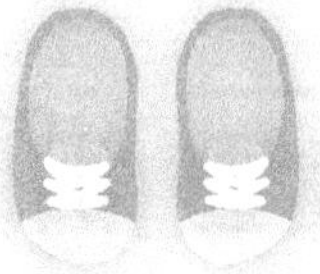

BEDTIME

- [ ] Clean Room 
- [ ] Bath Time 
- [ ] Put On Pajamas 
- [ ] Brush Teeth 
- [ ] Potty Time
- [ ] Read Book 
- [ ] Goodnight Kiss

MORNING

- ☐ Make Your Bed 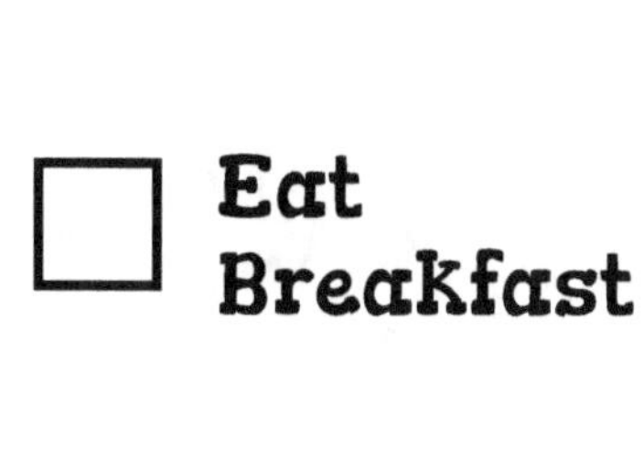
- ☐ Get Dressed 
- ☐ Eat Breakfast 
- ☐ Brush Teeth 
- ☐ Brush Hair 
- ☐ Get Backpack Ready 
- ☐ Put Shoes On 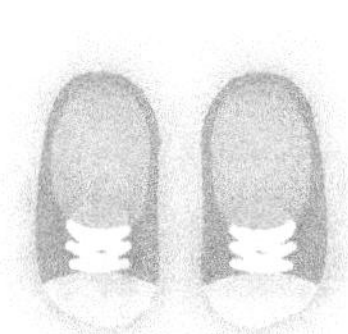

BEDTIME

- ☐ Clean Room 
- ☐ Bath Time 
- ☐ Put On Pajamas 
- ☐ Brush Teeth 
- ☐ Potty Time 
- ☐ Read Book 
- ☐ Goodnight Kiss 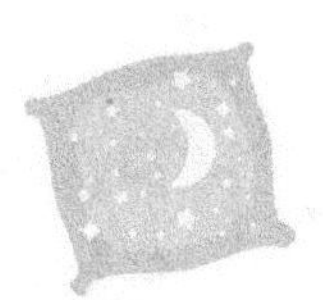

Today Is:______________

MORNING

- ☐ Make Your Bed 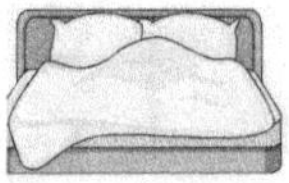
- ☐ Get Dressed 
- ☐ Eat Breakfast 
- ☐ Brush Teeth 
- ☐ Brush Hair
- ☐ Get Backpack Ready 
- ☐ Put Shoes On

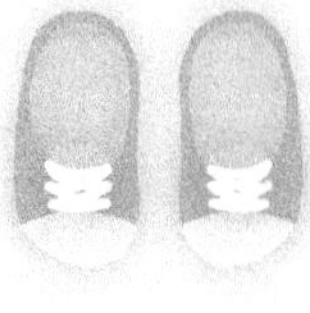

BEDTIME

- ☐ Clean Room 
- ☐ Bath Time 
- ☐ Put On Pajamas 
- ☐ Brush Teeth 
- ☐ Potty Time
- ☐ Read Book 
- ☐ Goodnight Kiss

Today Is:_______________________

MORNING

- ☐ Make Your Bed
- ☐ Get Dressed
- ☐ Eat Breakfast
- ☐ Brush Teeth
- ☐ Brush Hair
- ☐ Get Backpack Ready
- ☐ Put Shoes On

BEDTIME

- ☐ Clean Room
- ☐ Bath Time
- ☐ Put On Pajamas
- ☐ Brush Teeth
- ☐ Potty Time
- ☐ Read Book
- ☐ Goodnight Kiss

Today Is:_______________________

MORNING

- ☐ Make Your Bed 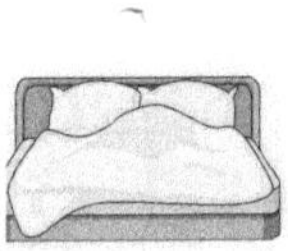
- ☐ Get Dressed 
- ☐ Eat Breakfast 
- ☐ Brush Teeth 
- ☐ Brush Hair
- ☐ Get Backpack Ready 
- ☐ Put Shoes On

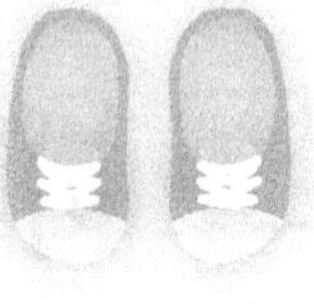

BEDTIME

- ☐ Clean Room 
- ☐ Bath Time 
- ☐ Put On Pajamas 
- ☐ Brush Teeth 
- ☐ Potty Time 
- ☐ Read Book 
- ☐ Goodnight Kiss

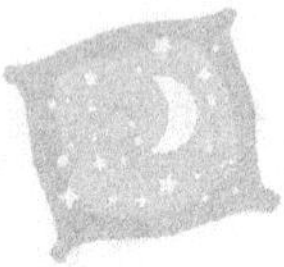

Today Is:_______________

MORNING

- [ ] Make Your Bed
- [ ] Get Dressed
- [ ] Eat Breakfast
- [ ] Brush Teeth
- [ ] Brush Hair
- [ ] Get Backpack Ready
- [ ] Put Shoes On

BEDTIME

- [ ] Clean Room
- [ ] Bath Time
- [ ] Put On Pajamas
- [ ] Brush Teeth
- [ ] Potty Time
- [ ] Read Book
- [ ] Goodnight Kiss

Today Is:_______________

MORNING

- ☐ Make Your Bed
- ☐ Get Dressed
- ☐ Eat Breakfast
- ☐ Brush Teeth
- ☐ Brush Hair
- ☐ Get Backpack Ready
- ☐ Put Shoes On

BEDTIME

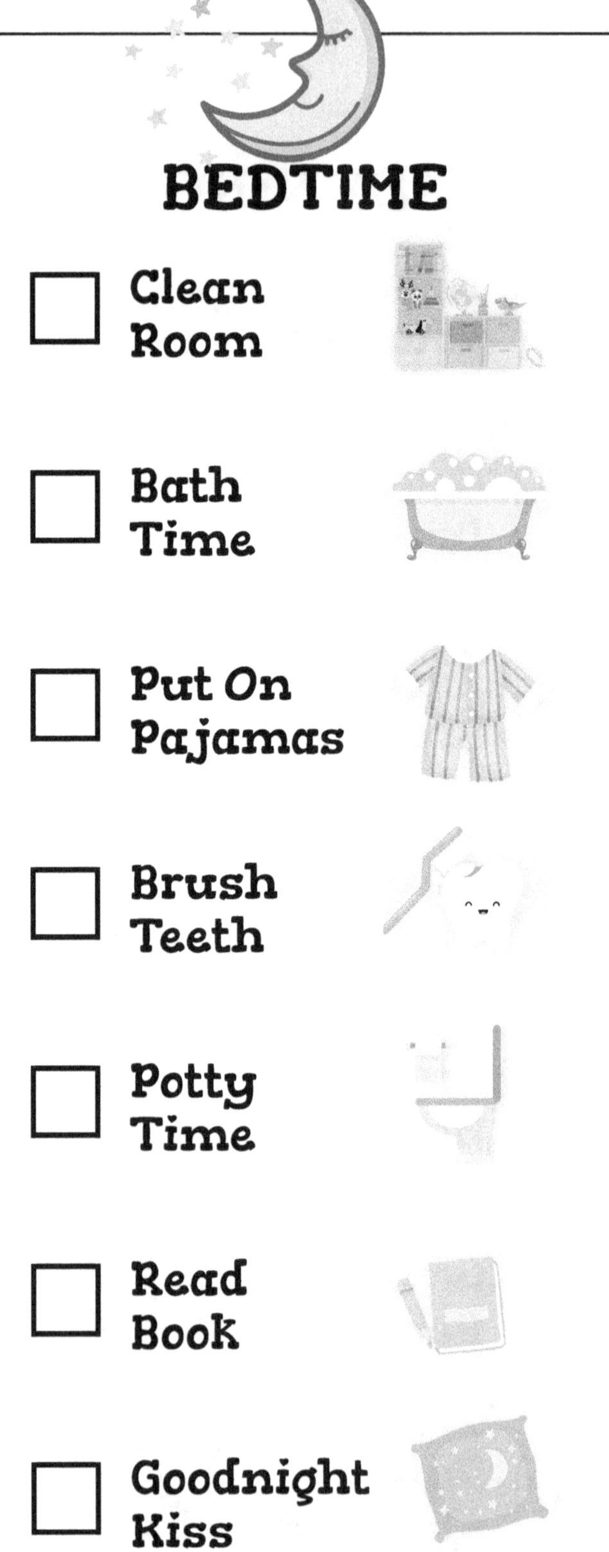

- ☐ Clean Room
- ☐ Bath Time
- ☐ Put On Pajamas
- ☐ Brush Teeth
- ☐ Potty Time
- ☐ Read Book
- ☐ Goodnight Kiss

Today Is:____________________

MORNING

- ☐ Make Your Bed
- ☐ Get Dressed
- ☐ Eat Breakfast
- ☐ Brush Teeth
- ☐ Brush Hair
- ☐ Get Backpack Ready
- ☐ Put Shoes On

BEDTIME

- ☐ Clean Room
- ☐ Bath Time
- ☐ Put On Pajamas
- ☐ Brush Teeth
- ☐ Potty Time
- ☐ Read Book
- ☐ Goodnight Kiss

Today Is:_______________

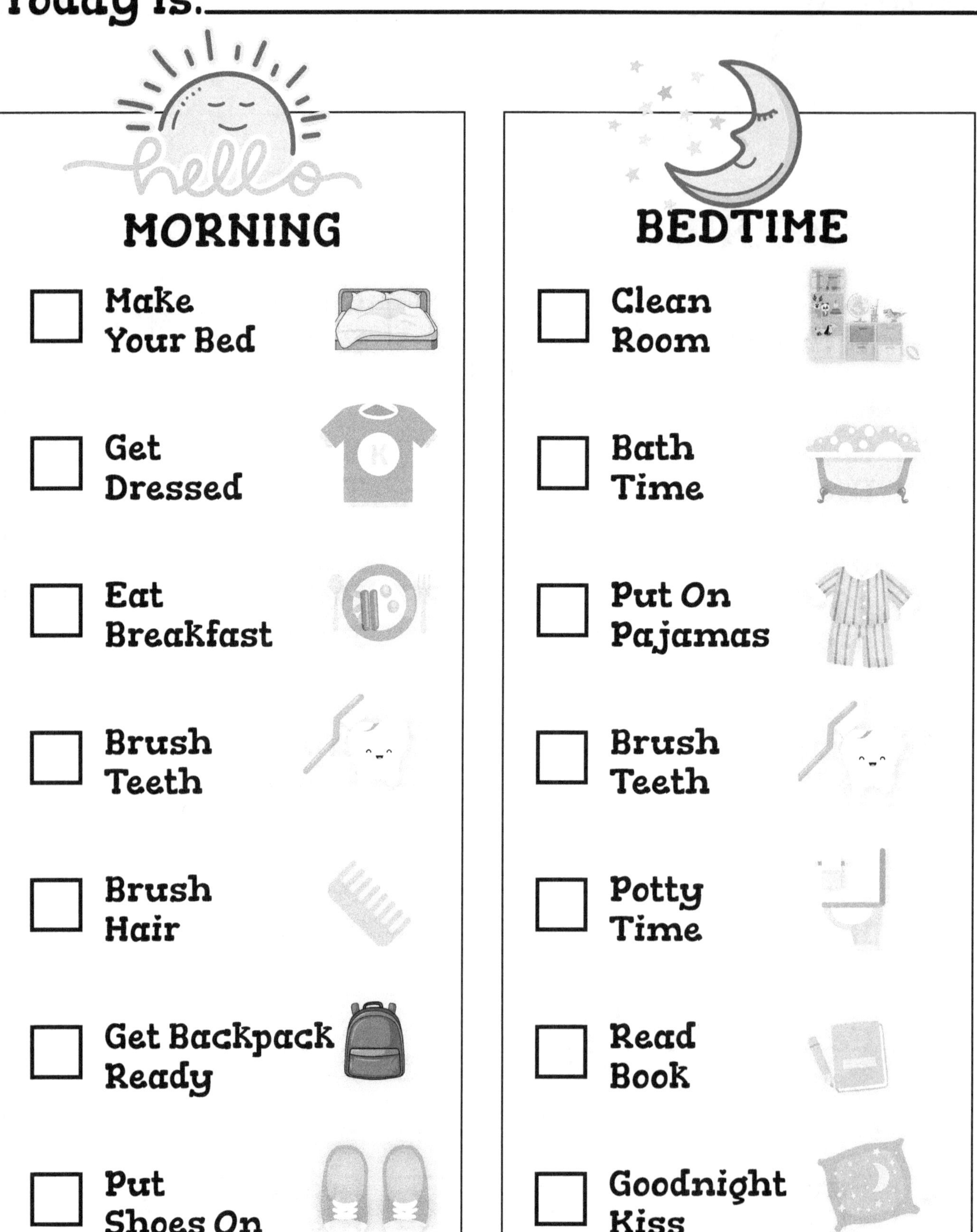

MORNING

- ☐ Make Your Bed
- ☐ Get Dressed
- ☐ Eat Breakfast
- ☐ Brush Teeth
- ☐ Brush Hair
- ☐ Get Backpack Ready
- ☐ Put Shoes On

BEDTIME

- ☐ Clean Room
- ☐ Bath Time
- ☐ Put On Pajamas
- ☐ Brush Teeth
- ☐ Potty Time
- ☐ Read Book
- ☐ Goodnight Kiss

Today Is:______________________

MORNING

- [ ] Make Your Bed
- [ ] Get Dressed
- [ ] Eat Breakfast
- [ ] Brush Teeth
- [ ] Brush Hair
- [ ] Get Backpack Ready
- [ ] Put Shoes On

BEDTIME

- [ ] Clean Room
- [ ] Bath Time
- [ ] Put On Pajamas
- [ ] Brush Teeth
- [ ] Potty Time
- [ ] Read Book
- [ ] Goodnight Kiss

Today Is:_______________

MORNING

- [ ] Make Your Bed
- [ ] Get Dressed
- [ ] Eat Breakfast
- [ ] Brush Teeth
- [ ] Brush Hair
- [ ] Get Backpack Ready
- [ ] Put Shoes On

BEDTIME

- [ ] Clean Room
- [ ] Bath Time
- [ ] Put On Pajamas
- [ ] Brush Teeth
- [ ] Potty Time
- [ ] Read Book
- [ ] Goodnight Kiss

MORNING

- ☐ Make Your Bed
- ☐ Get Dressed
- ☐ Eat Breakfast
- ☐ Brush Teeth
- ☐ Brush Hair
- ☐ Get Backpack Ready
- ☐ Put Shoes On

BEDTIME

- ☐ Clean Room
- ☐ Bath Time
- ☐ Put On Pajamas
- ☐ Brush Teeth
- ☐ Potty Time
- ☐ Read Book
- ☐ Goodnight Kiss

Today Is:_______________

MORNING

☐ Make Your Bed

☐ Get Dressed

☐ Eat Breakfast

☐ Brush Teeth

☐ Brush Hair

☐ Get Backpack Ready

☐ Put Shoes On

BEDTIME

☐ Clean Room

☐ Bath Time

☐ Put On Pajamas

☐ Brush Teeth

☐ Potty Time

☐ Read Book

☐ Goodnight Kiss

Today Is:_______________

MORNING

- ☐ Make Your Bed
- ☐ Get Dressed
- ☐ Eat Breakfast
- ☐ Brush Teeth
- ☐ Brush Hair
- ☐ Get Backpack Ready
- ☐ Put Shoes On

BEDTIME

- ☐ Clean Room
- ☐ Bath Time
- ☐ Put On Pajamas
- ☐ Brush Teeth
- ☐ Potty Time
- ☐ Read Book
- ☐ Goodnight Kiss

Today Is:_______________

MORNING

- ☐ Make Your Bed
- ☐ Get Dressed
- ☐ Eat Breakfast
- ☐ Brush Teeth
- ☐ Brush Hair
- ☐ Get Backpack Ready
- ☐ Put Shoes On

BEDTIME

- ☐ Clean Room
- ☐ Bath Time
- ☐ Put On Pajamas
- ☐ Brush Teeth
- ☐ Potty Time
- ☐ Read Book
- ☐ Goodnight Kiss

Today Is:________________________

MORNING

- ☐ Make Your Bed
- ☐ Get Dressed
- ☐ Eat Breakfast
- ☐ Brush Teeth
- ☐ Brush Hair
- ☐ Get Backpack Ready
- ☐ Put Shoes On

BEDTIME

- ☐ Clean Room
- ☐ Bath Time
- ☐ Put On Pajamas
- ☐ Brush Teeth
- ☐ Potty Time
- ☐ Read Book
- ☐ Goodnight Kiss

Today Is:______________

MORNING

- ☐ Make Your Bed 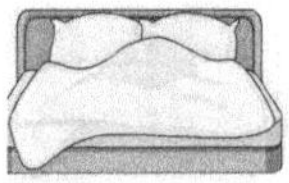
- ☐ Get Dressed 
- ☐ Eat Breakfast 
- ☐ Brush Teeth 
- ☐ Brush Hair
- ☐ Get Backpack Ready 
- ☐ Put Shoes On

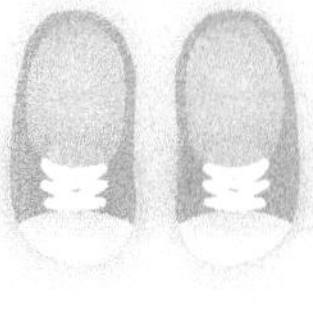

BEDTIME

- ☐ Clean Room 
- ☐ Bath Time 
- ☐ Put On Pajamas 
- ☐ Brush Teeth 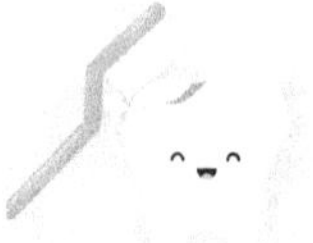
- ☐ Potty Time 
- ☐ Read Book 
- ☐ Goodnight Kiss